# LOVE MUST BE
# TOUGH

Other books by Dr. Dobson:

*Straight Talk to Men and Their Wives*
*What Wives Wish Their Husbands Knew about Women*
*Dare to Discipline*
*Hide or Seek*
*The Strong-Willed Child*
*Preparing for Adolescence*
*Emotions: Can You Trust Them?*
*Dr. Dobson Answers Your Questions*

# DR. JAMES C. DOBSON

*New Hope for Families in Crisis*

# LOVE MUST BE TOUGH

**WORD BOOKS**
PUBLISHER
WACO, TEXAS

A DIVISION OF
WORD, INCORPORATED

Scripture text marked NIV from The Holy Bible, New International Version, copyright © 1978 by the New York International Bible Society. Used by permission. Scripture quotations marked KJV are from the King James Bible.

Excerpt from *What Wives Wish Their Husbands Knew About Women* by Dr. James Dobson, published by Tyndale House Publishers, Inc., © 1975, used by permission; excerpts from *Dr. Dobson Answers Your Questions* by Dr. James Dobson, published by Tyndale House Publishers, Inc., © 1982 by Dr. James Dobson, used by permission.

ISBN 0-8499-0348-3
Library of Congress catalog card no.: 83-21785

Printed in the United States of America

*This book is dedicated to every person who has been rejected and wounded by a husband or wife on whom everything depended. I pray that these words will begin the healing process and provide a basis for genuine forgiveness to thrive. For only in forgiveness can peace be found.*

# Contents

*Introduction*                                    7

1. With Love to the Victims                      *11*
2. Panic and Appeasement                         *20*
3. The Tender Trap                               *30*
4. Young Love, True Love                         *38*
5. Opening the Cage Door                         *44*
6. The Tougher Questions                         *51*
7. The Valley of the Shadow                      *58*
8. Three Women Who Tried It                      *70*
9. Questions and Answers                         *75*
10. Victims of Affairs: A Dialogue               *98*
11. Discussion of the Dialogue                  *120*
12. Anatomy of Adultery                         *134*
13. Loving Toughness in Other Settings          *146*
14. Angry Women and Passive Men                 *176*
15. Loving Toughness for Singles                *183*
16. Components of a Good Marriage               *194*
17. With More Love to the Victims               *204*

# Introduction

"Sit down, Carol. I have to talk to you about something very serious. I know what I'm going to say will come as a shock to you, but I can't withhold the truth any longer. You deserve to know that I've been involved in an affair with a woman at the office for nearly eighteen months. Her name is Brenda and she is very attractive. It started as an innocent flirtation, but quickly progressed into something more—much more. Now we are unable to pretend any longer. That's why I've made an appointment with an attorney and I plan to divorce you as quickly as possible. I'm sorry! Honestly, I am. What more can I say? I never intended to hurt you. But I just don't love you any longer—and I *do* love Brenda—very deeply. So, Carol, I'm asking you to make it easy for both of us, and of course, for the kids. We'll all be better off as soon as this mess is settled."

With those words, the world falls off its axis for an unsuspecting woman and the children who can't understand why she cries. Suddenly, everything stable in their lives has been shattered. Rejection and insult are blended with pain and remorse. Self-esteem collapses like a grand old building scheduled for demolition. Security and confidence give way to fear and anxiety. The future loses its significance. But most disturbing of all, the woman who felt loved and respected a few hours before now feels utterly disdained and unlovable.

How common this set of circumstances has become in the Western world, not only for the Carols and Jeannies and Patricias around us, but also for the Robs and Toms and Carls. Whether for reasons of infidelity or because of one of the other great marriage killers, many husbands and wives find themselves being dragged relentlessly toward an unwanted divorce. For some, the realization does not come as a startling "announcement" like the one that shattered Carol. Rather, they watch helplessly as their marriages wither over a period of years, being consumed by an insidious cancer that gnaws at the soul of the relationship. They turn this way and that, searching desperately for answers— solutions—remedies. Unfortunately—and *this is the critical point*—the advice they are given by friends and even counselors is often disastrous in its effect.

The book you are about to read provides an alternative for those in the midst of family crises. My purpose in writing it has been to offer some practical tools—some understandings— which should be useful in drawing an apathetic husband or wife back in the direction of commitment. It may be surprising to learn that human conflict, *if properly managed,* can be the vehicle for transforming an unstable relationship into a vibrant, healthy marriage. On the other hand, the wrong response in moments of crisis can quickly smother the dying embers of love.

I should acknowledge at the outset that some of the principles I will offer may be controversial within Christian circles. It is my belief that the advice traditionally offered to victims of infidelity and other violations of trust has often been unbiblical and destructive. But obviously, not everyone will agree. To those who draw differing conclusions, I can only ask for charity as we seek to resolve the most difficult family problems with our limited knowledge and insight.

But that's enough for now. Let me offer one precaution before we proceed. If you are a husband or wife who is steadily losing the one you love—if you sense a growing disrespect and disdain from the most important person in your world—this book is intended for your eyes only. *Do not ask your partner to read it with you*. At least, you should review it first and then decide for yourself whether or not to reveal its message. It has been my experience that the principles of loving toughness are most effective when they are not discussed within the confines of a troubled marriage. I think you will soon understand why that is true.

Thank you for permitting me to share some new concepts with you. I hope you will find them helpful, even if you do not have a family in crisis.

# 1.

# *With Love to the Victims*

More than 45,000 letters and hundreds of telephone calls pour through our Focus on the Family offices each month, representing the full range of human circumstance and need. Every form of suffering and anguish, as well as many joys and triumphs, is shared with us in intimate detail from day to day. Included in that mail recently was a poignant letter from a man I'll call Roger.* His story moved me deeply.

A few months ago, my wife Norma left to go to the grocery store in a nearby shopping center. She told our four children that she would be back in half an hour and warned them to behave themselves. That occurred on Saturday morning. Six hours later she had not returned and I began a frantic search for her. I could imagine her being kidnapped or raped or even something worse. By Sunday morning I called the Detroit police, but they said they could not help until she had been gone 48 hours. The children and I were worried *sick!*

We requested prayer from our Church and Christian friends, especially for Norma's safety. She had left no notes or messages with friends, and she didn't call. We did find her car behind the shopping center, locked and empty. The police theorized that she had run

---

* All the letters quoted in this book have been modified to protect the names and identities of the writers.

away, but I didn't agree. That just wasn't like the woman I had lived with for fourteen years . . . the mother of my four children. We had been getting along quite well, actually, and had been planning to take a brief vacation over the Labor Day Weekend.

On Tuesday, I obtained the services of a well-known police detective and asked him to help us locate my wife—or at least discover what had happened to her. Well, he began interviewing her friends and associates and the details unfolded. To my utter shock, it became clear that Norma had left of her own free will with a married man from her place of employment. I just couldn't believe it.

Then about two weeks later, I got a "Dear John" letter, saying she didn't love me anymore—that our marriage was finished. Just like that, it was over. She said she would be returning in a few months to fight for the children, and that they would be living with her in Kansas.

Dr. Dobson, I tell you truthfully that I have always been a faithful father and husband. Even since my wife left, I have taken good care of the kids. I did the best I could to pull our lives together and keep going . . . to try to make a decent home for these four bewildered youngsters. Nevertheless, the court ruled in my wife's favor last month, and now I am alone.

I built our house a few years ago with my own hands, and now it is empty! All I have to show for the family I lost is a stack of Norma's bills and the memories that were born in these walls. My kids will be raised in an unchristian home, five hundred miles away, and I hardly have enough money to even visit them!

My life is a shambles, now. I have nothing but free time to think about the woman I love . . . and the hurt and rejection I feel. It is an awful experience. Norma has destroyed me. I will never recover. I am lonely and depressed. I wake up in the night thinking about what might have been . . . and what *is*. Only God can help me now!

I wish this letter from Roger represented a rare tragedy that occurred only in the most unusual of circumstances. Unfortunately, variations on this theme are increasingly common today. Sexual intrigue has become a familiar pattern in today's marriages, not only outside the framework of the Christian church but within it as well. And, of course, the most vulnerable victims of family instability are the children who are too young to understand what has happened to their parents.

That tragic impact on the next generation was graphically illustrated to me in a recent conversation with a sixth-grade teacher in an upper middle-class California city. She was shocked to see the results of a creative writing task assigned to her students. They were asked to complete a sentence that began with the words "I wish." The teacher expected the boys and girls to express wishes for bicycles, dogs, television sets and trips to Hawaii. Instead, *twenty* of the thirty children made reference in their responses to their own disintegrating families. A few of their actual sentences were as follows:

"I wish my parents wouldn't fight and I wish my father would come back. "

"I wish my mother didn't have a boyfriend."

"I wish I could get straight A's so my father would love me."

"I wish I had one mom and one dad so the kids wouldn't make fun of me. I have three moms and three dads and they botch up my life."

"I wish I had an M-1 rifle so I could shoot those who make fun of me."

I know it's hardly front page news to announce that the family is in trouble today, but it will always distress me to see little children like these struggling with such chaos at a time when simply growing up is a major undertaking. Millions of their peers are caught in the same snare. Consider the plight of Roger's children in the letter I shared. First, they lost their mother, then watched their father immersed in grief and agony, and finally found themselves jerked from familiar surroundings and transplanted into another state with a new guy who wanted to be called "Dad." They will never be the same! And why was this upheaval necessary? Because their mother cared more about her own happiness and welfare than she did about theirs. As a young woman, she had stood at an altar before God and man, solemnly promising to love and to cherish Roger—for better or worse, for richer or poorer, in sickness and health, forsaking all others, till separated by the hand of death. Unfortunately, Norma changed her mind.

It is apparent that the marriage between these former lovers is now beyond repair. But could it have been saved? Were there signs and symptoms that Roger failed to notice in the course of recent years? Would any advice by some profound "Solomon of psychology" have prevented the ultimate tragedy?

Before attempting to answer these important questions, let's consider another troubled family that has not yet passed the point of no return. Their difficulties are summarized in the following letter from a wife and mother whom I'll call Linda. Please give careful attention to this letter, for I will be referring to it throughout the remainder of this book.

Dear Dr. Dobson:
   I have a problem and it has become a terrible burden to me. It is affecting me both physically and spiritually. I grew up in a good Christian home, but married a man who was not a Christian. Paul and I have had a rough time—a lot of anger and fighting. He has refused to participate in the family as father of our three children— leaving everything up to me. He likes to bowl and watch football games on TV—and he sleeps all day Sunday. So things have always been rocky. But a much more serious problem arose a few years ago.
   Paul began to get interested in a beautiful divorcee who works as his bookkeeper. At first it seemed innocent, as he helped her in various ways. But I began to notice our relationship was deteriorating. He always wanted this other woman along whenever we went anywhere, and he spent more and more time at her house. He said they were doing accounting work but I didn't believe it. I began to nag and complain, and it just made him more determined to be with her. Gradually, they fell in love with each other, and I didn't know what to do about it.

I bought a book about this time in which the author promised if I'd obey my sinner husband, God wouldn't allow any wrong to happen so long as I was submissive. Well, in my panic, I thought I would lose him forever, and I agreed to let the other woman come into our bedroom with us. I thought it would make Paul love me more, but it just made him fall deeper in love with her.

Now he is confused and doesn't know which one of us he wants. He doesn't want to lose me and says he still loves me and our three kids, but he can't give her up, either. I love Paul so dearly and I have begged him to turn our problem over to the Lord. I love the other woman too and know she is also hurting, but she doesn't believe God will punish this sin. I have experienced terrible jealousy and pain, but I always put the needs of my husband and his friend above my own. But what do I do now? Please help me. I'm on the bottom looking up.

Linda

Have you ever been presented with a problem of this nature by either friend or relative? If so, what counsel have you offered? Do you think Linda handled the crisis appropriately? Would *you* have permitted your husband or wife to bring another lover into your bedroom in a last ditch attempt to save your crumbling marriage? Linda's motives seem clear enough. She knows that her husband just might leave her if she doesn't accommodate him in every way possible, and perhaps his escapade with the "beautiful divorcee" will blow over and be forgotten if she can avoid antagonizing him. And after all, doesn't the Bible say that "Charity [love] suffereth long and is kind; charity envieth not; charity vaunteth not itself, is not puffed up; doth not behave itself unseemly, seeketh not her own, and is not easily provoked" (1 Cor. 13:4, 5)? Love also "hopeth all things and *endureth all things*" (v. 7). Isn't it reasonable, therefore, for Linda to hold steady and "obey [her] sinner husband" in antici-pation of a miracle? Would you have agreed with the wisdom of this approach? Or would you have told her to divorce the bum and get him out of her life? Is there a third alterna-tive?

Based on my sixteen years of experience in marriage counseling, I am of the opinion that Linda's tolerance and longsuffering will probably be fatal to her marriage, and that her advisor has misinterpreted the Bible. If she deliberately set out to destroy what was left of her relationship with her husband, she could not do much more than has already been done. Though I empathize with her and intend no disrespect in this context, Linda has already made several fundamental mistakes that have contributed mightily to the present disaster in her home.

Linda's first error occurred in not recognizing the threat imposed by a beautiful divorcee. We must never underestimate the power of sexual chemistry existing between an attractive, needy, available woman and virtually any man on the face of the earth. In the case of Linda's husband, he suddenly found himself hopscotching between their two houses to provide whatever service the gorgeous-one might desire, while his wife concluded, "It seemed innocent." Innocent indeed! That's like a farmer thinking the fox visited his henhouse because he enjoyed the company of chickens!

Linda's second error occurred after observing that her marriage was going downhill. That was an extremely important moment in their relationship when an appropriate reaction from Linda might have pulled her playboy husband back from the precipice. But alas, she was ill prepared for the task. She nagged and complained. How inadequate but how human! Her husband was rapidly falling head over heels in love with "the other woman," and Linda's only response was hand wringing and verbal abuse. That form of reproof is about as effective with a wayward spouse as it is with a disobedient toddler: he doesn't even *hear* it!

The key word in the next phase of this story is *panic*. Linda could see the handwriting on the wall. It scrawled the frightening word *divorce* and moved on. How terrifying to one whose entire life is her family! She could visualize herself as the mother of three fatherless children, struggling to survive financially and emotionally in a lonely, broken home. Furthermore, she was losing the man she loved with all her being. And as panic is irrational, so was her reaction to it. She brought the other woman into her bedroom in a desperate attempt to occupy even a crowded corner of her husband's heart. What an incredible error in judgment! She soon discovered the inevitable result: "It just made him fall deeper in love with her."

The best news I can give Linda is that it is still possible for her to save her marriage, but she hasn't a minute to waste. Her husband has admitted that a spark of love still glows under the smoldering ashes ("He doesn't want to lose me and says that he still loves me and our three kids"), but she must not smother it! One more bad move and he will be gone forever. He is in a state of confusion and can be swayed one way or the other, but how can Linda tug him in her direction? She's tried everything in her own playbook and nothing has worked. What does she do now? If she is like so many others in today's world, she will be baffled by the question.

The frequency with which I have been confronted by problems similar to the plight of Linda and Roger has led me to write the book you are reading. I'm especially concerned about the person in an unsatisfying relationship whose mate could not seem to care less. Let me be more specific. In any apathetic or dying marriage, there is typically one partner who is relatively unconcerned about the distance between them, while the other is anxious or even panic-stricken over it. The detached spouse, whether husband or wife, may not realize how much danger the marriage is in or may not care. Therefore, that person resists any effort by his mate to entice him into counseling or compromises or even meaningful conversations to address their difficulties. "We have no serious problems," he contends.

The vulnerable partner, who could represent either sex but is more likely *initially* to be female, is aware that something precious is slipping away day by day. Everything of value is hanging in the balance, and she awakens in the midnight hours to contemplate the future. She thinks of the children—those beautiful kids who slumber unknowingly in their bedrooms— and wonders what will happen to them. She reaches for the affection and attention of her mate, and experiences depression when she doesn't get it.

I'm not implying, of course, that frail marriages can be blamed entirely on one spouse, and I'm accusing neither men nor women. Marital conflict *always* involves an interaction between two imperfect human beings who share the responsibility to one degree or another. Nevertheless, there is usually one partner who would do anything to hold the home together—and another who seems disinterested in the relationship.

The book you hold is dedicated, therefore, to that vulnerable member of the family who can be thought of as a victim in extreme cases. This is the only text of which I am aware whose primary purpose is to help a distressed person strengthen or preserve his or her marriage, *even in the absence of a willing spouse.* What advice can be offered to a woman like Linda whose husband is entangled in an affair, or a man like Roger whose wife seems to disrespect and hate him, or a wife whose husband is an alcoholic or drug abuser or child molester? And what about the woman who loves her husband and is loved by him in return, but worries about the total absence of romantic excitement between them? Is there any way she can heat up their relationship without nagging her husband incessantly?

Virtually every counseling program now in existence for such families is designed to bring together *two* people who can agree, at least, to discuss their problems. Or if therapy is offered for a single partner, it is directed at strengthening that individual to cope with the crisis and go it alone, if necessary. But our purpose here is unique: we want to help *one* spouse maximize the chances of preserving the marriage, as in Linda's case, and to survive till the long night is over. It's an ambitious undertaking.

In the process of reaching out to the hurting members of the family, it is my desire to accomplish much more. The principles I will describe are not only relevant to husbands and wives in a time of crisis; they are applicable to healthier marriages, too. Indeed, I wish they could be taught to every engaged or newlywed couple in the morning of their lives together. There would be fewer bitter divorces if young husbands and wives knew how to draw their drifting partners toward them, rather than relentlessly drive them away.

But the concepts I will share have even broader applicability than the interaction between husbands and wives. As we will see, they are relevant to *all* human relationships, including employers and employees, parents and children, pastors and parishioners, business and labor, guards and prisoners, Americans and Russians, and all the other categories of people who share an interface from time to time. In other words, I will be describing in subsequent chapters what I consider to be some universal concepts that cut across cultures, sexes, races and economic circumstances. And unless I have missed the mark, they will hit somewhere near your neck of the woods in one context or another.

Now isn't that just like an author to promise the moon to his readers? All writers have this tendency to overestimate the significance of their views. Books being published today offer everything from immeasurable wealth for men to instantly smooth thighs for women. Unfortunately, these authors rarely deliver on their promises; they remind me of "Professor Miraculous" in the Old West who sold his Elixir of Life from the back of his covered wagon and then left town . . . fast.

Hoping not to fall into the same "cure-all" trap, let me tell you candidly how I feel about the concepts you are about to read. Genuine insights into human behavior are not everyday occurrences—at least not for me. Indeed, if one stumbles onto two or three fundamental principles in the course of a lifetime, he has done well. The pages that follow focus on one of my allotted few. I've called the concept *love must be tough.* It won't smooth out your thighs or make you wealthy, but it should help you cope better with the people around you.

# 2.
# *Panic and Appeasement*

**O**nly those who have been rejected by a beloved spouse or lover can fully comprehend the tidal wave of sorrow that crashes into one's life when a loss is threatened. Nothing else matters. There are no consoling thoughts. The future is without interest or hope. Emotions swing wildly from despair to acceptance and back again. If one word must be selected to describe the entire experience, it would be something equivalent to *panic.*

Since panic is the characteristic response to rejection, imagine how much more distressing a loss is felt when a new and perhaps younger lover is brought into the picture! *Nothing* in human experience can compare with the agony of knowing that the person to whom you pledged eternal devotion has betrayed your trust and is now engaged in sexual intimacies with a "stranger" . . . a competitor . . . a more beautiful or handsome playmate. Death itself would be easier to tolerate than being tossed aside like an old shoe. Those who have experienced such a loss tell me that the most painful aspect is their own loneliness—knowing that their unfaithful partner is comforted in the embrace of another. How desperately Christian counsel is needed by those who awaken to the awful knowledge that adultery has taken residence in their homes!

In the absence of that guidance, a rejected man or woman often reacts in ways that make matters worse. Just as a drowning person exhausts himself in a desperate attempt to grasp anything that floats, including his rescuer, the panic-stricken lover typically tries to grab and hold the one who is attempting to escape. I have witnessed the scenario a thousand times. Supercharged emotions zip up and down a roller coaster of extremes.

Upon disclosure that the marriage (or premarital relationship) is over, the first reaction is almost sure to be one of utter shock and disbelief. That is followed by weeping and wailing and gnashing of teeth, giving way to begging and pleading for forgiveness and restoration. When that too is rejected, a bargaining period ensues. The person promises to be a better lover, to be more considerate, to quit work or to go to work or to bring flowers more often or to have a baby or whatever is perceived to be important to the disenchanted mate. Suggestions are made that they both seek counseling assistance, but the offer is almost always declined by the one whose mind is already settled. Then when all negotiations prove futile, an angry stage is often entered, perhaps eliciting every mean and hostile thought that the victim has harbored. A man may threaten to inflict bodily harm on his ex-lover during this phase, and sometimes succeeds in doing so. With or without violence, the hostility of this terrible ordeal is ventilated in a period of wrath, ending in physical and emotional exhaustion. Then a brief time of acceptance occurs, after which grief and sorrow return like an unwelcome visitor who so recently came to call. Finally, the cycle repeats itself on a revolving merry-go-round of misery.

With the reader's indulgence, I will continue to include letters that illustrate the circumstances I am attempting to describe. It is the best way I know to make the words come to life. These are the thoughts and feelings of real people who have been through the turbulent waters I have described. Faye is such a person whose panic has led her to plead and bargain with her husband. She wrote:

Dear Dr. Dobson:
I'm writing to you regarding my marriage. My husband gave me the bad news earlier this year, telling me he no longer loved me. He told me of his plans to leave soon. Well, I begged and

pleaded with him to stay with me, and he did for a while. Then one night he became so cruel and said many mean things before walking out.

Ever since he left, for some odd reason, I humiliate myself every time I see him. I beg him to call the kids and me. He'll say, "I don't want to talk to you!" I tell him how much I love him, and he'll reply, "I have no love for you! I don't hate you, but I don't love you either." That hurts me so much!

I've asked Joe to see a counselor but he said he doesn't need any help from anyone. He doesn't even care about the marriage. He only wants his freedom. He says he wants to go to Pennsylvania where he can get a better job in the mining business.

So what do you think the problem is? We've been married eleven years and we have two beautiful children. The odd thing is that we never did fight or argue very much. It just seems that he slowly turned against me and changed his mind about being my husband. Have you ever seen cases such as this?

Now something awful has happened. I went to the doctor recently and he told me I'm going to have to have surgery on my eyes and I could lose my vision. I'll be going into the hospital next week. I just couldn't help it, Dr. Dobson. I broke down and called my husband again, but he was indifferent to the news. He quietly asked me if I had made any arrangements for the kids and if I had someone to take me to the hospital. I asked if he would take me and then stay in the waiting room while I had the surgery. Joe hesitated and then said, "Well, I guess so."

What must I do to get Joe to love me again? He has told me over and over that nothing could make him care for me like before. I have cried and begged him to come home. I've told him how badly we need him. I've tried being nice. That doesn't help either. I've told him I'm afraid and I need him especially now and he says, "I'm sorry. The timing is bad."

Is it likely that we will end up in a divorce? Joe has asked for one but I've refused. I still have hopes that we can get back together. I told him that and he said, "Can't you get it through your head that I'll never love you again?"

We used to do everything together, but now it's all over. I keep calling my husband because if I don't, he would never call me. Next Monday is a holiday; he didn't ask what the kids and I were doing, so I asked if he would spend the day with us. He acted so smart and said, "If I have *nothing* else to do . . ." Should I ignore him? If I do, I'll never see him again.

Dr. Dobson, please help me. Tell me what to do. I love Joe so much!

Faye

Though I understand the compulsion that drives Faye to plead for Joe's attention and love, she is systematically destroying the last glimmer of hope for a reconciliation. She has stripped herself of all dignity and self-respect, crawling on her belly like a subservient puppy before her master. The more Joe insults her and spurns her advances, the more intensely she seems to want and need him. That is, in fact, the way the system works.

The message Faye is giving her husband can be summarized thus: "Oh, Joe, I need you so badly. I can't make it without you. I spend my days waiting for you to call and am crushed when the phone doesn't ring. Won't you please, please, let me talk to you occasionally? You see, Joe, I'll take you any way I can have you—even if you want to walk all over me. I am desperate here without you."

Linda, whose letter I shared in the first chapter, has given precisely the same message to her unfaithful husband. In her case, however, the panic even led her to invite the other woman into her bedroom. What a pitiful expression of low self-esteem and inadequacy. My heart aches for her and for the millions of others facing similar sorrows.

Linda and Faye have brought us now to an extremely important and well-known principle of human relationships: *panic often leads to appeasement, which is virtually never successful in seeking to control the behavior of others.* In fact, it often leads directly to war, whether between husbands and wives or between antagonistic nations. Attempts by one side to "buy off" an aggressor or offender appear to represent peace proposals, but they merely precipitate further insult and conflict. World War II might have been prevented and fifty million lives saved if British Prime

Minister Neville Chamberlain and other national leaders had understood the folly of appeasement in 1936–39. Every time they offered Adolph Hitler another Czechoslovakia to tranquilize his lust for dominion, they only fed his disdain for them and their armies. Hitler's interpretation of their yearning for "peace in our time" as evidence of weakness and fear enticed him to ever greater audacity. Finally, it became necessary to fight what Winston Churchill called the most *preventable* war in modern times. That is where appeasement leads, whether in affairs of state or affairs of the heart.

In Linda's case, her husband threatened to divorce her if she didn't allow him to engage in extramarital intimacies in their bedroom. Not only was this a cruel form of blackmail; it was also a test of her confidence and self-respect. She failed it.

Let me make it clear that my opposition to marital appeasement—this defenseless, pleading reaction—has nothing to do with pride, as such. If stripping oneself of dignity would preserve a marriage, I would enthusiastically endorse the behavior. Unfortunately, the opposite is true. *Nothing* destroys a romantic relationship more quickly than for a person to throw himself, weeping and clinging, on the back of the cool partner to beg for mercy. That infuses the wayward spouse with an even greater desire to escape from the leech that threatens to suck his life's blood. He may pity the wounded partner and wish that things were different, but he can rarely bring himself to love again under those circumstances.

Perhaps the reader can now understand why I disagree strongly with Christian leaders who recommend that rejected husbands and wives smile during a time of breakup or unfaithfulness and act as though nothing had happened. This advice is especially characteristic of those who write books for women today. They recommend, "Just keep lovin' your men, ladies, and sooner or later they'll come to their senses." As you will recall, that counsel was offered to Linda by some misguided author who promised, "God [won't] allow any wrong to happen so long as [you are] submissive." That is Pollyanna in the pulpit if I've ever heard it!

Please understand that I believe firmly in the Biblical concept of submission, as described in the Book of Ephesians and elsewhere in Scripture. But there is a vast difference between being a confident, spiritually submissive woman and being a *doormat*. People wipe their feet on doormats, as we know. Furthermore, it is terribly destructive to one's internal organs to hold inside all the sadness and anxiety generated during a disintegrating marriage. Everything from hypertension to ulcers and even cancer can result from unventilated stress.

Finally, successful marriages usually rest on a foundation of *accountability* between husbands and wives. They reinforce responsible behavior in one another by a divinely inspired system of checks and balances. In its absence, one party may gravitate toward abuse, insult, accusation and ridicule of the other, while his or her victim placidly wipes away the tears and mutters with a smile, "Thanks, I needed that!" This passivity was the subject of a recent country song entitled "She's Got To Be A Saint." The words tell us what often happens to the appeaser who lacks the courage to confront a disrespectful partner.

I'm out late ev'ry night, doin' things that ain't right,
    And she'll cry for me.
When I'm down in the dumps and she nurses my lumps,
    How she cries for me.
And she'll never complain, she keeps hiding the pain
    But I know all the while:
She's not feeling too well 'cause I've put her thru hell;
    Still she forces a smile.
She's got to be a saint, Lord knows that I ain't.
I finally realized right before my eyes,
    Here is a saint.

There's a dress in the shop that'll make her eyes pop
    But she'll look away.

She'd-a gotten a lift if I bought her that gift
     For her birthday.
But her birthday has come and I feel like a bum
     'Cause I spent my last dime
On a worthless old friend on a drunken weekend.
     I've done it time after time.
She's got to be a saint, Lord knows that I ain't.
I finally realized right before my eyes,
     Here is a saint.

Should I stay, should I go? I really don't know,
     My mind's in a blur.
Soon it's gonna be dawn and if she finds me gone
     Would it be best for her?
I see her cry in her sleep so I kiss her wet cheek
     I kneel by her and pray.
And I'll turn off the light, step out in the night,
     and I'll go on my way.
She's got to be a saint, Lord knows that I ain't.
I finally realized right before my eyes,
     Here is a saint.*

Nice guy, huh? He's just the kind of jerk that every father fears is going to marry his daughter. (I can't help wondering what he said to the Lord in that bedside prayer.) But let's take a closer look at him. What would motivate a man to be so cruel? Every elementary psychology book describes the yearning for affection that throbs within the breast of all mankind, males and females alike. Yet here we see a drunken bum who sneaks away from the caring, sharing, loving devotion of this marvelous woman. Why does he want to escape in the night? His wife would do anything to hold him, yet he prefers to spend the weekend weaving on some barstool with another wasted sot. How can such strange behavior be explained? Well, in addition to the effects of booze, this bleary-eyed crooner just can't handle

---

an appeasing wife who gives him everything and requires nothing in return. Sober or not, *very few of us can!*

It is even more important to understand the behavior of the woman represented in this song. Is she really some kind of superhuman saint? Of course not! She is merely a vulnerable female who has considered the alternatives and concluded that her only option is to keep her mouth shut. Perhaps in younger years she stood toe to toe with this beer-drinking bully and was hurt more than he by the brawl. Or maybe she is by temperament a peace-lovin' lady who just can't tolerate conflict. Either way, she knows that her husband is on the verge of leaving, and she wants to give him no excuse to split. Therefore, she has chosen to appease her man in the hope that he will clean up his act.

What passes for a "saint" to a half-drunk husband, then, is a normal woman who is carefully concealing what she really feels. You can be *certain* that she is in agony. She's like a duck who is calm and serene above the water but paddles like crazy below it. How can we be so sure that she is in secret pain? First, because contented people do not cry themselves to sleep at night, and second, because of the delicate psychological nature of human beings. Our emotional apparatus is like a finely tuned violin which can be distorted so easily. The woman in the song is being abused by the one she loves, and there is no doubt that she is experiencing agitation, resentment, low self-esteem and other disturbing emotions. These kinds of troubling feelings simply cannot be denied in most people, especially the female of the species.

The question remains, what is she going to do with these negative emotions? Sending them downward into a secret holding tank is the psychological equivalent of storing TNT. Sooner or later, a spark will touch off a blast that will make Mt. St. Helens look like a popgun. (Helens was a saint, too, as you recall!) If marriage is to last a lifetime, then it must not accumulate and preserve resentments that can eventually turn into hatred. There must be a mechanism for releasing small tensions as they arise in everyday life.

In the absence of that safety valve, what will happen to the saint in the course of time? Let's assume that her alcoholic husband stays with her but continues to take advantage of her passivity. A blowup is likely at some future moment. To illustrate the point, let's look in on our saint twenty years downstream, cleverly described in the lyrics of another country song entitled "To Daddy."*

Mama never seemed to miss the finer things in life.
If she did, she never did say so to daddy.
She never wanted to be more than mother and a wife.
If she did, she never did say so to daddy.
The only thing that seemed to be important in her life
Was to make our house a home and make us happy.
Mama never wanted any more than what she had.
If she did, she never did say so to daddy.
He often left her all alone;
But she didn't mind the stayin' home.
If she did, she never did say so to daddy.
And she never missed the flowers
And the cards he never sent her.
If she did, she never did say so to daddy.
Being took for granted
Was a thing that she accepted,
And she didn't need those things to make her happy.
And she didn't seem to notice that he didn't kiss and hold her.
If she did, she never did say so to daddy.
One morning we awoke, just to find a note
That mama carefully wrote and left to daddy.
And as he began to read it,
Our ears could not believe it,
Words that she had written there to daddy.

---

* Written by Dolly Parton. Copyright © 1976 Velvet Apple Music, 8 Music Square West, Nashville, TN 37203. All rights administered by Tree Pub. Co., Inc. International Copyright Secured. All Rights Reserved. Used by permission.

She said the kids are old enough, they don't need me very much,
And I've gone in search of love I need so badly.
I have needed you so long,
But I just can't keep holding on.
She never meant to come back home.
If she did, she never did say so to daddy.
Goodbye to daddy.

# 3.
# *The Tender Trap*

*I* hope we have succeeded in documenting three conclusions thus far:

1. Marital (and premarital) conflict typically involves one partner who cares a great deal about the relationship and the other who is much more independent and secure.
2. As a love affair begins to deteriorate, the vulnerable partner is inclined to panic. Characteristic responses include grieving, lashing out, begging, pleading, grabbing and holding; or the reaction may be just the opposite, involving appeasement and passivity.
3. While these reactions are natural and understandable, they are rarely successful in repairing the damage that has occurred. In fact, such reactions are usually counterproductive, destroying the relationship the threatened person is trying so desperately to preserve.

In the previous chapter we explored the fears and sorrows reverberating in the mind of the rejected partner. Now let's take the next step by looking at the husband or wife who is drifting away. In order to pull that person back from the brink, we need to understand the forces operating within. What do *you* believe motivates a man or woman to terminate a marriage? What thoughts are typical of one who rejects the unconditional love offered at home? What secrets lie deep within the psyche of the woman who has an affair with her boss, or the man who chases the office flirt? Is desire for a new thrill the only enticement, or are more basic motivators operating below the surface?

It has been my observation that the lust for forbidden fruit is often incidental to the real cause of marital decay. Long before any decision is made to "fool around" or walk out on a partner, something basic has begun to change in the relationship. Many books on this subject lay the blame on the failure to communicate, but I disagree. The inability to talk to one another is a *symptom* of a deeper problem, but it is not the cause itself. The critical element is the way one spouse begins to perceive the other and their lives together. It is a subtle thing at first, often occurring without either partner being aware of the slippage. But as time passes, one individual begins to feel trapped. That's the key word, *trapped.*

In its more advanced stages, a man considers his wife (gender is interchangeable throughout these discussions) and thinks these kinds of thoughts: "Look at Joan. She used to be rather pretty. Now with those fifteen extra pounds she doesn't even attract me anymore. Her lack of discipline bothers me in other areas, too—the house is a perpetual mess and she always seems totally disorganized. I hate to admit it, but I made an enormous mistake back there in my youth when I decided to marry her. Now I have to spend the rest of my life—can you believe it—all the years I have left—tied up with someone I'm disinterested in. Oh, I know Joanie is a good woman and I wouldn't hurt her for anything, but man! Is this what they call living?"

Or Joanie may be doing some thinking of her own: "Michael, Michael, how different you are than I first thought you to be. You seemed so exciting and energetic in those early days. How did you get to be such a bore? You work far too much and are so tired when you come home. I can't even get you to talk to me, much less sweep me into ecstasy. . . . Look at him, sleeping on the couch with his mouth hanging open. I wish his hair wasn't falling out. Am I really going to invest my entire lifetime in this aging man? Our friends don't respect him anymore and he hasn't received a promotion at the plant for more than five years. He's going nowhere and he's taking me with him!"

If Joanie and Michael are *both* thinking these entrapment thoughts, it is obvious that their future together is in serious jeopardy. But my point is that the typical situation is unilateral. *One* partner begins to chafe at the bit without revealing to the other how his perception has evolved. A reasonably compassionate person simply does not sit down calmly and disclose these disturbing rumblings to someone who loves him. Instead, his behavior begins to change in inexplicable ways.

He may increase the frequency of his evening business meetings—anything to be away from home more often. He may become irritable or "deep in thought" or otherwise noncommunicative. He may retreat into televised sports or fishing trips or poker with the boys. He may provoke continuous fights over insignificant issues. And of course, he may move out or find someone younger to play with. A woman who feels trapped will reveal her disenchantment in similar indirect ways.

Let's examine a letter from a woman whose husband quite obviously feels locked into his marriage. He's never asked for a divorce, but we can sense what he is thinking from what his wife tells us.

Dear Dr. Dobson:
  I have been married for twenty-one years and the entire trip has been stormy. My husband cares about only one thing: getting ahead. He works two jobs, seven days a week. I know he loves our four kids, but he has no time for them, or else he's too exhausted to give them any attention.
  Our relationship is stale! My husband has never (and I do mean

*never!*) approached me physically with a hug, kiss or embrace, but will "go along with it" if I am the initiator. I long to get inside his head and find out how he feels, but he simply won't talk about personal things.

We went to a marriage counselor a few years ago after almost splitting up, and I thought he was really helping us. Jack didn't agree. He called the counselor "worthless" and a "waste of money." Now he says he'll see a divorce attorney before he'll ever go back.

I've studied 1 Peter 3 (about submission) until I'm blue in the face. I've practiced those principles to the best of my ability. What has Jack done in response? He now *expects* me to always be cheerful and loving, regardless of how he treats me. *Am I to accept this nonaffectionate man forever* [author's italics] or is there hope for change? He enjoys putting me down.

I love him but sometimes I get so upset that I think I hate him. He just withdraws. Do you have any suggestions or books or tapes that could help me? Jack won't read anything I give him.

Thanks for your help.

Nancy

How could it be said any more clearly? Here we have a man who obviously disrespects his wife, treating her like an unwanted child. I would bet my shirt he's wishing there were an acceptable way out of his commitments and obligations. On the other side we hear an emotionally deprived woman asking, "What's going on in this man's mind? Why is he so cold and unresponsive?" The answer? He feels trapped.

This intense desire to escape from a marriage can occur on the first day of the honeymoon or fifty years thereafter. For men, it is *the* primary ingredient of a midlife crisis. But these feelings of constraint are by no means unique to men. For women, they usually (but not always) occur in response to an unromantic relationship that refuses to be energized. A wife may "reach" for her husband for years, beg for his attention, nag him when he fails to notice, and then scream to herself, "Help! I'm suffocating in this loveless marriage! Somebody get me out!"

How sad it is, furthermore, that this trapped partner who is fighting an impulse to run is rapidly sinking deeper and deeper into a form of marital quicksand. Why? Because the more he struggles to gain his freedom (or even secure a little breathing room), the more his panic-stricken spouse clutches his neck. Even the fluctuating emotions of the rejected party are interpreted as attempts to grab and hold him. For example:

> *The response of grief*: "Please don't hurt me. Come and meet my needs."
>
> *The response of anger*: "Get back in line, stupid! How dare you try to walk out on me!"
>
> *The response of blame*: "How could you do this to me and the kids?"
>
> *The response of appeasement*: "Name it and you can have it. Just don't leave me."
>
> *The response of servility* (*the doormat*): "No matter what you do, I'll go on smiling 'cause you're mine."

The common denominator between these varied responses is one of entrapment. They each restrict the freedom of the less interested party. For someone in the trapped syndrome, love then becomes an *obligation* rather than an incredibly wonderful privilege. Perhaps it is now obvious why the natural reaction of the panic-stricken spouse typically drives the cool partner farther away; the more he pulls back from their relationship to gain desired space, the tighter the bonds close around him. He sometimes becomes almost claustrophobic in his desperate attempts to breathe—to get the noose off his neck. He may even resort to infidelity as a vehicle to escape from his partner's clutches.

If the reader will forgive the redundancy, I'll make a more graphic attempt to express this important concept. I have often explained it to those I have counseled by demonstrating with my hands, as follows:

Partners A and B decide to get married and live happily ever after. At some point along the way, however, Partner B begins to feel trapped in the relationship. His spouse offends or bores him in numerous ways, and he resents those five constraining words, "'til death do us part."

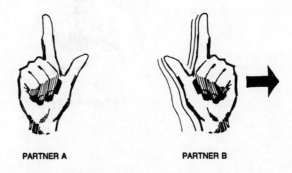

In order to deal with this sense of containment—this restriction of freedom—Partner B moves gradually to the right, away from Partner A.

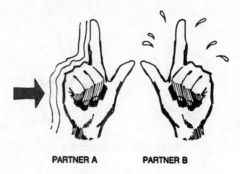

PARTNER A          PARTNER B

Partner A observes Partner B's retreat and reacts with alarm. Her impulse is to pursue Partner B, closing the gap even tighter than before.

PARTNERS A AND B

Partner B makes more obvious attempts to flee, but in a moment of desperation, Partner A jumps on Partner B and clutches him with all her strength. Partner B struggles to escape and will surely run the moment he gains release.

PARTNER A

Partner A then droops in loneliness, wondering how something so beautiful became so sour.

## INSTEAD . . .

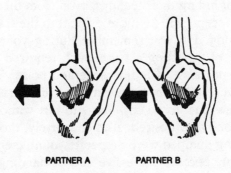

PARTNER A          PARTNER B

Regardless of what common sense tells us to the contrary, Partner A's best chance of attracting and holding a suffocating lover is to pull backward slightly, conveying freedom for Partner B and respect for herself in the process. Curiously, Partner B often moves *toward* Partner A when this occurs.

We've all observed this need for "space" in human relationships, but the concept is still difficult to comprehend when it pertains to ourselves and our loved ones. The next chapter will explain why.

# 4.

# *Young Love, True Love*

**W**e've been discussing psychological principles that may appear vague and esoteric when considered in adult terms. Grownups have a way of hiding their feelings, even from themselves. Perhaps these concepts will be more evident in the transparency of the very young. Do you remember during your dating days that the task of attracting a prize catch required a certain reserve—an appearance of indifference and poise? Those of our peers who were most successful in romantic pursuits were the cats who knew how to be coy—how to flirt without appearing to need the one they desired. And conversely, those who were eternally being dumped were desperate young men and women who inevitably became possessive and demanding—calling on the phone six straight times and parking the car in the shadows to spy on the lover, then complaining bitterly the next day about who the lover was with the night before. That was the beginning of the end, leading directly to what we used to call "the maroon harpoon."

Today's adolescents use different language to describe splintering romances, but the rules to the game have not changed. Lovers' quarrels typically involve one "clinging vine" who is being axed and an "oak tree" that stands confidently above the fray.

But who are these lady-killers and heartbreakers who seem

so independent and secure? Do they take satisfaction in shredding their former boyfriends and girlfriends? Most do not. They are merely self-centered individuals who love to pursue but hate to be caught. They throw themselves into the chase with abandon as long as the affair is new and challenging. But their interest melts like hot ice cream the moment they achieve their goal and capture the prize. Suddenly, the tables are turned. They are needed—possessed—depended upon. Demands are made on them for loyalty and service and commitment. Thenceforth, their only passion is for escape and freedom.

One reason I'm so familiar with these characteristics of young love is that I have such a good memory. It seems only yesterday that my wife, Shirley, and I were playing these cat-and-mouse games. In a subsequent chapter I will describe how I kept her guessing about my feelings for nearly two years, and even ended the relationship a time or two. If that seems cruel to a pretty little college sophomore, you should know that Shirley had broken more hearts than Bluebeard himself. As a teenager, she was interested in boys only until the moment she caught them. Then it was curtains. In her wake lay a trail of fallen adolescent heroes who made the mistake of trying to possess her—to hold her and demand her allegiance. They soon heard "the closing of the door" as she was on her way out.

One young man named Stan took his notice of termination quite hard. He and Shirley were sitting in his car at the edge of a park during their senior year of high school. After telling him that they were through, Stan sat staring at the angora dice hanging from his mirror for a few minutes. Then he bolted from the car and disappeared into the night. Shirley had no idea where he had gone or whether he would come back. Stan returned in about ten minutes with a bloody handkerchief wrapped around his hand, telling her that he had socked a tree in his anger. Oh, the joys and sorrows of adolescence!

Teenage romance is often humorous to adults because its passions are so raw and undisguised. I suppose that's why I enjoy listening to the words of songs currently popular among the young. As with country and western music, the values of today's youth are clearly audible within the horrid lyrics of disco and rock.

Consider the following lament by a teenager whom I'll call Harry Highschool. His best friend has just snagged the last perfect woman on the face of the earth. Harry calls her "Jessie's Girl."

Jessie is a friend
Yeah, I know he's been a good friend of mine
But lately something's changed
It ain't hard to define.
Jessie's got himself a girl,
And I wanna make her mine.
And she's watchin' him with those eyes,
And she's loving him with that body
I just know it.
And, he's holding her in his arms late, late at night.
You know I wish that I had Jessie's girl.
I wish that I had Jessie's girl.
When can I find a woman like that?
I'll play along with the charade.
There doesn't seem to be a reason to change.
You know I feel so dirty when they start talkin' cute.
I wanna tell her that I love her,
But the point is prob'ly moot.
And I'm looking in the mirror all the time.
Wonderin' what she don't see in me.
I've been funny.
I've been cool with the lines.
Ain't that the way love's supposed to be?
Tell me, when can I find a woman like that?
You know, I wish that I had Jessie's girl.
I wish that I had Jessie's girl.
I want Jessie's girl. *

Have you ever read lyrics that better reflected the adolescent mindset than these? Notice the depth of Harry's understanding of true love; he thinks it should flow like a river to any cool dude who's funny with the lines. He would like to tell Jessie's girl that he loves her, but admits he'd settle for *any* girl "like that." He's in love with an image—an illusion—not a woman. Observe his unconcealed sexual fantasies and jealousies and passions. When young love is viewed from this perspective, it's not surprising that 50 percent of all teenage marriages end in divorce within five years.

There is little doubt that adolescent romance is typically selfish and introspective; it blanches and buckles when asked to sacrifice or contribute or give. The most intense spasms of desire are felt by those who, like Harry, pursue sex objects that appear unreachable, unattainable. We should ask what would happen if Harry should be so fortunate as to capture his elusive princess? What if she fell for him heart and soul, writing love letters every day and begging for his attention? What if she blasted Harry every time he looked longingly at a new unattainable doll? I can tell you with great certainty that the bubble would soon burst. Harry would gladly give this complaining chick back to Jessie.

Harry will not always be so flighty in his sexual pursuits. Maturity should bring greater stability to his relationships with the opposite sex. But let me make this extremely important point, of relevance to us all: Adult romantic relationships continue to bear many of the characteristics of adolescent sexuality. We differ from the young only in degree, and will always reflect the rudiments of earlier sexual attitudes and values. Thus, grownups still love the thrill of the chase, the lure of the unattainable, the excitement of the new and boredom with the old. Someone wrote, "Men love women in proportion to their strangeness to them." It is true. In committed love, of course, these immature impulses are controlled and minimized, but they exist nonetheless, especially in males. Futhermore, the desire for "breathing room" that was so typical during adolescence will be a lifelong characteristic, as will be the need to feel fortunate to have "captured" the one we married.

Conversely, in marriage where the mystery and dignity have not been preserved in the relationship, or where one partner clings to the other in desperation, the couple is faced with a serious "balance of payments" deficit. All the emotional energy flows in one direction, which is certain to deplete reserves and resources. This is precisely what happens when an insecure spouse begins to smother the other. Even if infidelity and abandonment are never threatened, the pleading by one partner for the affection and attention of the other serves to short-circuit the electrical attraction between them. Once the process begins that says, "I own you!" the game is over. The home team loses.

Human freedom is a precious thing and we react decisively against those who would restrict it or take it from us. Not even a lover can deprive us of that God-given freedom *unless we surrender it voluntarily.* In fact, not even God will attempt to take it. If you ever come to Him in a love relationship, I guarantee that it will be of your own choice and through no coercion on His part. Not only *must love be tough*—it must be *free*, as well!

Country singer Tom T. Hall wrote a song in which he revealed surprising insight into this aspect of male-female relationships. He said, "If you hold love too loosely then it flies away; if you hold love too tightly, it'll die. It's one of the mysteries of life."* Hall's observation is accurate. If the commitment between a man and a woman is given insufficient importance in their lives, it will wither like a plant without water. The whole world knows that much. But fewer lovers seem to realize that extreme dependency can be just as deadly to a family. It has been said that the person who needs the other *least* will always be in control of the relationship. I believe that to be true.

Returning now to the letters from Linda and Faye, we can

---

* "It's One Of The Mysteries Of Life." Written by Tom T. Hall. Published by Hallnote Music. Copyright 1977. All rights reserved. Used by permission.

begin to see what probably went wrong during their season of panic. Please understand that I'm not laying the blame for their husbands' departures on these women whose only crime was loving their men. But it is likely that they each played an unwitting part in the conflict, first by denying sufficient space to their self-centered husbands, and finally by choking their necks when they tried to leave. There *must* be a more effective way to draw cool lovers to the warmth of the hearth.

# 5.

# *Opening the Cage Door*

**W**hen married persons find themselves hurtling relentlessly toward a divorce, they sometimes turn to marriage counselors, ministers, psychologists and psychiatrists to stem the tide. The counsel they are subsequently given often involves changes in the way the two partners relate to one another from day to day. It may be proposed that they reserve an evening each week as "date night," or that they alter their sex habits or workaholic lifestyles. Such advice can be helpful in reestablishing communication and understanding between two wounded and disappointed people, but it may be inadequate to save a dying marriage. Why? Because the counsel is directed at *surface* issues.

In most troubled marriages, a basic problem lies ominously below these relatively minor irritants. It involves the way one party has begun to perceive the other, as we have described. When expressed in materialistic terms, it is the value ascribed to one human being by another. That perceived worth is incorporated in the word *respect,* and it is absolutely basic to all human relationships.

The way we behave from day to day is largely a function of how we respect or disrespect the people around us. The way employees perform is a product of how they respect the boss. The way children behave is an outgrowth of their respect for their parents. The way nations coexist is directly attributable to their respect for one another. And certainly, the way husbands and wives relate is a function of their mutual respect and admiration. That's why marital discord *almost always* emanates from seething disrespect somewhere in the relationship! That is the *bottom line* of romantic confrontation.

What I've been trying to describe are those gradual changes in perception—that subtle deterioration in attitude—that precede marital conflict. A starry-eyed young man and woman agree to wed because they hold one another in awe—in deepest respect. And if they choose to remain for a lifetime, it will be because that positive attitude has been maintained, or in its absence, from the sheer power of commitment. Either way, the quality of their relationship will be a direct product of their mutual respect through the years.

Perhaps it is now apparent where the present line of reasoning is leading us. If there is hope for the dying marriages we have examined, and I certainly believe there is, then it is likely to be found in the reconstruction of *respect* between warring husbands and wives. Can there be any doubt that Linda's husband thoroughly disrespects his wife? Of all forms of disdain that one individual can show for another, there is none more profound than blatant infidelity. That is the *pits* in human affairs. And though Faye and Nancy are not yet victims of unfaithfulness, they share the same basic problem. Their husbands feel trapped in suffocating relationships with women they clearly disrespect.

We return now to the question with which we began: what can be done to preserve these three marriages and the millions of others they represent? *The answer requires the vulnerable spouse to open the cage door and let the trapped partner out!* All the techniques of containment must end immediately, including manipulative grief, anger, guilt and appeasement. Begging, pleading, crying, hand-wringing and playing the role of the doormat are equally destructive. There may be a time and place for strong feelings to be expressed and there may be an occasion for quiet tolerance. But these responses must not be used as persuasive devices to hold the drifting partner against his or her will.

To the reader who is desperately in need of this advice, please pay close attention at this point: I'm sure you would not have dreamed of using these coercive methods to convince your husband or wife to marry you during your dating days. You had to lure, attract, charm, encourage him or her. This subtle game of courtship had to take place one delicate step at a time. Can you imagine what would have occurred if you had wept violently and hung on the neck of your lover saying, "I think I'll die if you don't marry me! My entire life amounts to nothing without you. Please, please! Oh, please don't turn me down," etc.

That approach to a potential marriage partner is about as disastrous as it would be for a used car salesman. What do you think he would accomplish by telling a potential customer through his tears, "Oh, please buy this car! I need the money so badly and I've only had two sales so far today. If you turn me down, I think I'll go straight out and kill myself!"

This is a ridiculous analogy, of course, but there is linkage in it. When one has fallen in love with an eligible partner, he attempts to "sell himself" to the other. But like the car dealer, he must not deprive the buyer of free choice in the matter. Instead, he must convince the customer that the purchase is in his own interest. If a person would not buy an automobile to ease the pain of a salesman, how much more unlikely he is to devote his *entire being* to someone he doesn't love, simply for benevolent reasons. None of us is that unselfish. We are permitted by God to select only one person in the course of a lifetime with whom to invest everything we possess, and few of us are willing to squander that one shot on someone we merely pity! In fact, it is very difficult to love another person romantically and pity him or her at the same time.

Let's apply this concept to married life. If begging and pleading are ineffective methods of attracting a member of the opposite sex during the dating days, why do victims of bad marriages use the same groveling techniques to hold a drifting spouse? They are only increasing the depth of disrespect by the one who is escaping. Instead, they should convey their own version of the following message when the right time affords itself:

"John, I've been through some very tough moments since you decided to leave, as you know. My love for you is so profound that I just couldn't face the possibility of life without you. To a person like me who expected to marry only once and to remain committed for life, it is a severe shock to see our relationship begin to unravel. Nevertheless, I have done some intense soul searching, and I now realize that I have been attempting to hold you against your will. That simply can't be done. As I reflect on our courtship and early years together, I'm reminded that you married me of your own free choice. I did not blackmail you or twist your arm or offer you a bribe. It was a decision you made without pressure from me. Now you say you want out of the marriage, and obviously, I have to let you go. I'm aware that I can no more force you to stay today than I could have made you marry me in 1972 [or whenever]. You are free to go. If you never call me again, then I will accept your decision. I admit that this entire experience has been painful, but I'm going to make it. The Lord has been with me thus far and He'll go with me in the future. You and I had some wonderful times together, John. You were my first real love and I'll never forget the memories that we shared. I will pray for you and trust that God will guide you in the years ahead."

Slowly, unbelievably, the trapped spouse witnesses the cage door vibrate just a bit, and then start to rise. He can't believe it. This person to whom he has felt bound hand and foot for years has now set him free! It isn't necessary to fight off her advances—her grasping hands—any more.

"But there must be a catch," he thinks. "It's too good to be true. Talk is cheap. This is just another trick to win me back. In a week or two she'll be crying on the phone again, begging me to come home. She's really weak, you know, and she'll crack under pressure."

It is my *strongest* recommendation that you, the rejected person, prove your partner wrong in this expectation. Let him marvel at your self-control in coming weeks. Only the passage of time will convince him that you are serious—that he *is* actually free. He may even test you during this period by expressions of great hostility or insult, or by flirtation with others. But one thing is certain: he will be watching for signs of weakness or strength. The vestiges of respect hang in the balance.

If the more vulnerable spouse passes the initial test and convinces the partner that his freedom is secure, some interesting changes begin to occur in their relationship. Please understand that every situation is unique and I am merely describing typical reactions, but these developments are extremely common in families I have seen. Most of the exceptions represent variations on the same theme. Three distinct consequences can be anticipated when a previously "grabby" lover begins to let go of the cool spouse:

1. The trapped partner no longer feels it necessary to fight off the other, and their relationship improves. It is not that the love affair is rekindled, necessarily, but the strain between the two partners is often eased.
2. As the cool spouse begins to feel free again, the question he has been asking himself changes. After having wondered for weeks or months, "How can I get out of this mess?" He now asks, "Do I really want to go?" Just knowing that he can have his way often makes him less anxious to achieve it. Sometimes it turns him around 180 degrees and brings him back home!

Let me illustate the effect of this second consequence in another way. Have you ever had something strike you funny at a formal banquet or church service or funeral, where it would have been humiliating to laugh out loud? Just the fact that you *couldn't* snicker made you jerk and snort to hold in the belly-laugh. This happened to me in a college chapel service many years ago. I was in a mischievous mood and I put a small ball of aluminum foil on my knee. I intended to fire it twenty rows or more toward the front. Instead, I flipped it straight into the ear of a shy student sitting directly in front of me. He rose about six inches from his seat, and then settled down without ever looking back. His ear immediately began to glow and pulsate to the rhythm of his heart, which struck me funny. In fact, my roommate and I became hysterical, despite the seriousness of the service. He leaned to his left and covered his mouth and I tilted to the right. We crowded extraneous thoughts through our heads in a desperate attempt to gain control. But just when we thought the crisis had passed, we would notice again the red spot spreading down the lad's neck in the direction of his shoulder. By this time one half of his head was crimson and the other white. That's all it took for the snorting and snuffing to begin again. It was awful. People all around us were disgusted with our irreverence, and who knows what the guy with the throbbing ear was thinking. But I'll tell you honestly, it was impossible to stop laughing.

Finally, the speaker finished his heavy message and the benediction was said. Everyone stood and the victim took his ear and walked out without making a comment. The pressure was over and it was acceptable to laugh at last. But suddenly, there was nothing funny. The very fact that we could guffaw if we wished to removed the need even to smile. This is the way we humans are constructed. And that's the way claustrophobic lovers feel when they are suddenly released. They often lose their need to escape.

3. The third change occurs not in the mind of the cool spouse but in the mind of the vulnerable one. Incredibly, he feels better—somehow more in control of the situation. There is no greater agony than journeying through a vale of tears, waiting in vain for the phone to ring or for a miracle to occur. Instead, the person has begun to respect himself and receive small evidences of respect in return. Even though it is difficult to let go once and for all, there are ample rewards for doing so. One of those advantages involves the feeling that he has a plan—a program—a definite course of action to follow. That is infinitely more comfortable than experiencing the utter despair of powerlessness that he felt before. And little by little, the healing process begins.

By this point in our discussion, some of my readers are undoubtedly beginning to ask a question that means more to me than any other aspect of the work we are doing: Is the advice offered herein consistent with Scripture? It is certainly different from what many Christian leaders would recommend.

If I felt that my recommendations contradicted Biblical teachings I would never utter them again. God's Word is the standard for all human behavior and values. And in this context, there are specific passages that support the psychological conclusions I have drawn. The most relevant is found in 1 Corinthians 7:12–15, NIV. Note especially the portion I have italicized.

> If any brother has a wife who is not a believer and she is willing to live with him, he must not divorce her. And if a woman has a husband who is not a believer and he is willing to live with her, she must not divorce him. For the unbelieving wife has been sanctified through her believing husband. Otherwise, your children would be unclean, but as it is, they are holy. *But if the unbeliever leaves, let him do so. A believing man or woman is not bound in such circumstances; God has called us to live in peace.*

Those seem like very straightforward instructions to me. The Apostle Paul was talking to men and women who were married to unbelievers—some of whom who were undoubtedly involved in bad marriages. He was telling them unequivocally that divorce was not an option. Period. They were instructed to remain faithful and try to win their unchristian spouses to the Lord. Good counsel! But Paul was also sensitive to those who had no choice in the matter. Like Linda and Faye, they were unable to hold their partners at home. In those instances they were advised to let the partners go. There is no blame in accepting a fate beyond their control. And just as I have indicated, this acceptance of the inevitable will result in "peace." Here we see the marvelous wisdom of the Creator as expressed through His servant in interpersonal and psychological dimensions.

# 6

# The Tougher Questions

**W**e have dealt with the matter of letting go of a disenchanted lover. But in real-life situations, marital problems often involve complications and entanglements that make our task more difficult. Let's return, for example, to those men and women who know their spouses are being unfaithful. What should be the attitude of Linda and the other hurting people whose partners are fooling around? Whereas their infidelity would likely have been hidden a century ago, today it may be blatantly admitted and defended by the guilty. A recent popular song illustrates this justification of evil.

### Torn Between Two Lovers*

There are times when a woman has to say what's on her mind,
Even though she knows how much it's gonna hurt.
Before I say another word, let me tell you, I love you.
Let me hold you close and say these words as gently as I can.
There's been another man that I've needed and I've loved.
But that doesn't mean I love you less. [ *Oh, really?* ]**

---

\* © 1976 Muscle Shoals Sound Publishing Co., Inc. and Silver Dawn Music, Inc. Written by Phillip Jarrell and Peter Yarrow. All rights reserved. Used by permission.
\*\* Author's comment.

And he knows he can't possess me and he knows he never will.
There's just this empty place inside of me that only he can fill.
Torn between two lovers, feelin' like a fool.
Lovin' both of you is breaking all the rules.

You mustn't think you failed me just because there's someone
     else.
You were the first real love I ever had and all the things I
     ever said,
I swear they still are true. [*How about the marriage vows?*]*
For no one else can have the part of me I gave to you.
Couldn't really blame you if you turned and walked away.
But with everything I feel inside, I'm askin' you to stay.
Torn between two lovers, feelin' like a fool.
Lovin' both of you is breaking all the rules.

Isn't that sweet? This little darlin' is sleeping with two men
and one of them is not her husband. That's bad enough. Then
she has the utter audacity to tell the man she married that her
affair will be continuing. He has two choices in the matter:
live with it or shove off. He wasn't even asked for his opinion.
She was determined to have her cake and ice cream too, or if
her husband preferred, she'd settle for ice cream—with the other
lover.

How about it, now? What would your answer be to this proposition? The question is highly relevant to our discussion. Linda's
husband has confronted her with the same dilemma. She wrote,
"He is confused and doesn't know which one of us he wants.
He doesn't want to lose me and says he still loves me and
our three kids, but he can't give her up either."

There is no shortage of husbands and wives who are torn
between two (or more) lovers. I could fill the balance of this
book with letters and living illustrations of men and women
like Linda whose mates are openly engaged in sexual escapades.
They, like the writer of the following letter, ask the same question: "What do I do now?"

---

* Author's comment.

Dear Dr. Dobson:

I heard your radio program today when you urged frustrated people not to get a divorce. It seemed like you were talking directly to me. But if I'm not going to get a divorce, then what can I do? Every day is worse than the one before and my husband and I are farther apart. I am more depressed than I've ever been.

My husband and I are thirty-four years old and we have four children. Chuck no longer cares about the things he used to love. He used to sing in the choir in church and work on a camper he was building for the family. Now he seems to be looking for a whole new way of life, spending his time dancing in bars and discos. He is involved with other women, spending money we can't afford, but nothing satisfies him for long. Tell me, what would *you* do if you were me?

My husband says I'm too old-fashioned, too moral. But I'm trying to live a Christian life. He says he would rather die than be a Christian. He makes me feel so dirty!

How do I continue this? I ask you. How?

A friend in Christ,
Mabel

Let's turn to the Christian literature to find answers to Mabel's question. Listed below are five suggestions which were paraphrased from *actual* books offering counsel to female victims of infidelity. This passive approach has been the "party line" for several decades, not only in books but also in the advice offered by Christian counselors, pastors, relatives and friends. Let me ask you to put yourself in Mabel's situation as you read these recommendations.

1. After you learn of your husband's infidelity, go to him and tell him again how much you love him. Tell him you don't intend to let him go, and indeed, that you plan to fight for him. Your persistence will tell him that *there might be a chance that you will shape up.*

2. Tell your husband that you understand what he's done, and indicate that you realize you have given him some

reason to fool around. Do not label his behavior sinful or immoral.

3. Ask God to reveal your specific failures that have led to your husband's unfaithfulness. When the answer comes, take this list of shortcomings to your husband and review it with him. Tell him specifically how you think you may have contributed to his need to find another lover and ask for his forgiveness.

4. Don't expect quick improvement in your relationship with your husband. Your marriage has taken years to get into the mess it's in, and it may take as long to recover. In the meantime, don't ask your husband to stop seeing the other lover.

5. Continue treating your husband as the man of the house. Remind him he is still your husband and the father of your children. If he is not living at home, encourage him to eat his meals with you and the children any time he wants to. Let him know you are ready to meet his sexual needs whenever he comes over.

Certainly, what is recommended here seems like the loving, nonjudgmental thing to do, and in fact, I agree that these suggestions will be entirely appropriate *after* a reconciliation has occurred. There will be a time for total forgiveness, no mention of the past, admission of personal flaws and shared responsibility for the problems that developed. Love demands nothing less. Furthermore, we must acknowledge that there *are* occasions when "unconditional acceptance," as described above, can be successful in winning back a wayward spouse. I have seen women who permitted their husbands to abuse them, betray them, deprive them and insult them, yet who returned such love and kindness that the marriage was saved. It *does* occur. The personality and temperament of the abusing partner is the critical factor here, of course.

Nevertheless, I must report the facts as I see them. *A passive approach often leads to the dissolution of the relationship.* It is especially destructive in marriages where the unfaithful partner is desperate to escape from the wife he thoroughly disrespects, yet who won't let him go and instead announces her intention of fighting for him (see item 1 above) no matter what he does to gain his freedom.

Let me make one more attempt to explain why appeasement, even in the name of Christianity, can prove fatal to a marriage. Just as toddlers and teenagers will challenge the authority of their parents precisely for the purpose of testing their confidence and courage, a husband or wife will sometimes do the same. They, like children, want to feel the security of loving discipline which says, "Go this far and no farther." There is safety in defined limits for human beings of all ages.

In other books I have described what happens when a parent collapses in response to consistent challenges from a child. Respect is lost when the question is asked, "How tough are you?" and the answer comes back, "I'm made of Jell-O!" Not only does the child begin to feel that the parent is unworthy of his respect, but he senses a lack of love in the relationship, too. Genuine love *demands* toughness in moments of crisis. It's true for grownups, too.

As indicated above, adults will occasionally challenge one another for the same reasons they challenged their parents as children. Unconsciously, perhaps, they are asking the question, "How much courage do you have, and do you love me enough to stop me from doing this foolish thing?" What they need in that moment is loving discipline that forces them to choose between good and bad alternatives. What they don't need, contrary to the suggestions offered above, is permissiveness, understanding, excuses, removal of guilt and buckets of tender loving care. To dole out that kind of smother-love at such a time is to reinforce irresponsibility and generate disrespect. It deprives the marriage of *mutual accountability!*

Let's look at a couple of specific examples. Suppose a teenager comes home, stoned on amphetamines. He sits in his room for days at a time, popping pills while he deteriorates physically and emotionally. So what should his parents do? Does the adolescent need understanding and rationalization and never a word about his problem? Should his parents tell him how *they've* caused his addiction by their many failures? Is it best that they prop up his life and purchase his narcotics for him? Certainly not. *Love must be tough!* If they cannot reason with him and encourage him to get help, they should force the issue to a crisis that will save him from himself. By whatever method, including painful confrontation, they must break the cycle of behavior that is destroying their son and get him to seek professional help.

How about the example of a wife whose husband is an alcoholic? Should she "cover" for his drunken condition, lying to his boss and concealing the problem from the neighbors? No, that is the *worst* course of action for a victim of alcoholism. The best approach is to force a crisis that will bring the matter to a head. Then it can be treated and resolved. (We will discuss this matter in greater detail in subsequent chapters.)

Perhaps my point has been made. Infidelity is an addiction that can destroy a life as quickly as drugs or alcohol. Once a man or woman is hooked on the thrills of sexual conquest, he or she becomes intoxicated with its lust for pleasure. This person needs every available reason to go straight—to clean up his life. He certainly does not need a spouse who says dreamily, "I understand why you need the other woman, David. My goodness! I am so riddled with flaws that it's no wonder you went looking for someone else. You should see the list of my own stupidities that I'm keeping. Let me propose a course of action: You just go on with your other friendships for a few years while I work on myself, and maybe you'll eventually feel like being a husband again. Spend our money foolishly if you wish, and I'll get along somehow. Maybe I can take in ironing or do some babysitting. In the meantime, drop over and I'll meet your needs anytime you wish. Bring your dirty clothes and a big appetite, too. The kids and I will try to keep the conversation from getting too heavy for you because we sure wouldn't want you to get the notion that you're doing something wrong. And David, why don't you bring your ladyfriend with you the next time you come. I'll bet she's a sweetheart."

That approach is like buying booze for the drunk and drugs for the junkie. It is *weak* love! It is disastrous!

I hope I've made the case for the use of loving toughness in response to blatant rebellion and sin. But the question remains, *how* is that discipline implemented? Does the offended party scream and cry and throw things? Does he or she run to the nearest telephone to call the attorney? Is it time to play dirty, spreading gossip that will embarrass and hurt the rascal? No! No! No! Those approaches may be tough, but they aren't loving!

I'll offer an alternative in the next chapter.

# 7.
# *The Valley of the Shadow*

**A**nyone who has tried to diet or stop smoking or maintain an exercise program for more than two weeks knows just how difficult it is to eliminate well-entrenched patterns of behavior. We can fight our persistent old habits tooth and nail, but they're always lurking out there somewhere, threatening to return and subject us again to their servitude. Many of these behavioral characteristics were cut during childhood in channels that run deep and wide. To change our ways of responding now, as adults, requires us to dam up the river, dig new basins and reroute the flow. It may be the most difficult thing a person is ever asked to do.

That is what the adulterer or the alcoholic or the child abuser is facing. When approached rationally, he will tell us that he dislikes what he has become and wishes he could change. But the old patterns persist, leading him to do tomorrow what he did yesterday. His promises and his declarations are not worth the gunpowder required to blow them up.

How, then, can we help turn him around? What can Linda do to make her husband abandon his female toys? She has tried nagging and begging and being sweet and being angry, but nothing has worked. What now?

Well, if Linda were sitting in my office, I would first suggest that we make her marital problems a matter of concerted prayer.

*Any* personal crisis should begin at that point, especially when it involves something so important as the stability of a family. Let me make it clear that the advice offered in this book or any other (except the Bible) is mere human wisdom, and is woefully inadequate without the direct leadership of the Holy Spirit. In almost every troubled marriage, there is a spiritual dimension that cannot be brushed aside by the application of psychological principles alone, regardless of how brilliant they sound.

Furthermore, in talking to hundreds of Christians who have seen their families torn apart, I have heard one comment with overwhelming consistency: "I would never have made it without the Lord!" They have then told me how the presence of Jesus Christ was never more real and compassionate than during the worst of the storm, when the winds of tragedy howled around them. It is my privilege, therefore, to direct Linda and all the multitudes who suffer into this harbor of God's infinite love. I have seen Him turn disaster into triumph, healing wounds and repairing hopelessly shattered relationships.

But it is also true that God often uses pain and crisis to bring a sinful person to his senses. There is something about great stress that takes us back in the direction of responsibility. Remember that the rebellious Prodigal Son decided to go home to daddy only when his money ran out and he was eating with the pigs. A daily serving of slop does tend to make one hunger for the fatted calf. In the context of the present discussion, there is a place for a deliberately conceived confrontation in a troubled marriage that may take it literally to the door of death.

For purposes of illustration, let me return to Linda's situation. At the appropriate moment and armed with the prayer I have described, I would urge her to precipitate a crisis of major proportions. She must give Paul a reason for wanting to reroute his river. He is unlikely to make the investment of energy and self-control to accomplish that task until he absolutely must. It is only when he becomes miserable that he will accept the responsibility for change. It is only when he sees everything of

value to him—his home, his children, his wife, his reputation—
begin to slip away that his choices will become clear. It is
only when the well runs dry that Paul will begin to miss the
water.

You see, Linda's husband needs her to be tough—but loving—at this moment, perhaps more than any other time in his
life. He is wavering between responsibility and irresponsibility,
admitting that he's confused as to which path he should pursue.
He needs a strong excuse to do the right thing, and he almost
seems to be asking Linda to give him that motivation. As long
as he is permitted to be "torn between two lovers," he can
postpone a commitment and play one "wife" against the other.
That shatters everyone involved.

Unfortunately, Linda is overdue in providing the motivation
that Paul needs. It should have come like a clap of thunder
the first time he fooled around. I stated earlier that it is not
too late for her marriage to be saved, but I can't be certain
of that fact. Linda's power to draw Paul back has been depleted
by the missed opportunities she has squandered. Let me explain
why. Whenever sexual indiscretion is occurring, a marital relationship necessarily deteriorates with the passage of time. It is
inevitable! Therefore, the influence that a husband or wife holds
with which to pull the partner back from the brink is rapidly
seeping away. That's why in instances of infidelity, it is necessary
to fire your biggest guns as early in the affair as possible.

What I'm saying is that an early blowout is better than a
slow leak! The chances of saving a marriage will never again
be as great as they are after the first indiscretion. Remember
that Linda's husband *gradually* fell in love with the other woman.
That slowly developing love would not have been possible if
Linda had said to him on the occasion of his third trip to the
divorcee's house: "Paul, you are putting a severe strain on our
marriage and I strongly suggest that you hear what I'm saying.
If you persist in visiting this girl, you will come home and
find me and the kids gone." If he paid no heed, she should
deliver on the promise.

I can hear someone saying, "I thought you didn't recommend divorce." I don't, and I'm not. The choice will rest with the unfaithful partner. But it must be clear to him that he cannot have it both ways. It simply won't work. And in fact, the best thing that can happen to a tomcat who prowls around at night is to come home after his first escapade to face reality. Right then, in the aftermath of his foolishness, he needs to feel the full impact of his sin. He should sit in an empty bedroom thinking, "What have I done? What in the world have I gone and done? I have violated the trust of this beautiful woman who has borne my children, devoted herself to my happiness, cared for me when I was ill, and loved me more than I ever deserved. And, in return, what does she get but a selfish cad who would sneak around behind her back and sleep with someone else? Will she ever forgive me? Will my children forgive me? Will *God* forgive me? Can I ever forgive myself?"

It would be naïve, of course, to assume that this contrite repentance is so easily achieved. It may be months before an affair is discovered, and even when loving toughness is applied, the confrontation between husband and wife is rarely a simple encounter. Games of bluff are played, skirmishes are fought, battles are won and lost. It can be a bloody engagement, even within the context of love. That is why I recommend that the victim—the one who is trying desperately to hold things together—never head for such a crisis without the guidance of a Christian professional who can help steer the course. Whenever I am assisting a vulnerable man or woman through these turbulent waters, I make myself available by phone both night and day to encourage them and help manage the conflict. I also request the prayerful support of every believer who knows and loves the family that is under fire.

Even in these difficult relationships where the fury of hell itself is unleashed on the more responsible partner, there are rewards for hanging tough. Remember that the basic marital problem usually involves matters of respect, which are often generated during instances of confrontation. I can't explain why this is true of human nature, but I know that it is. I learned that lesson when I was in high school.

I had just moved to a small Texas city in my junior year of high school and attended a football game the first Friday night. Since I knew no one, I sat among unfamiliar students in the stadium. I must have looked like an easy mark to an eleventh-grader named Ellis, who sat behind me and repeatedly hit me on the head with his rolled-up program. After two or three verbal exchanges between us, I turned around and jumped on his belly. I pounded him on the head and shoulders while he flailed at my body. It was a typical high school free-for-all with very little damage done to either of us. But believe it or not, that was the prelude to a deep and lasting friendship between Ellis and me. It was based on mutual respect. I overheard him telling another student in the hall later that year, "I wouldn't mess with Dobson. He doesn't look like a fighter but he's tough as nails." My other bosom buddy from the same era was a 180-pound senior named Harlan with whom I slugged it out one Saturday morning. That fight ended in a bloody draw, but again, it precipitated genuine admiration between Harlan and me.

Applying this concept to romantic affairs now, the same characteristic is often evident. How frequently it happens that a dating couple will become engaged or will rush toward marriage shortly after recovering from the worst fight in their history together. I am *not* recommending that Linda, Faye, Nancy, Mabel and the others try to blow their husbands over with anger or hit them with frying pans. I am saying that by having the courage to stand up for themselves, they may regenerate a portion of the respect they have lost.

Finally, let's return to the problem of the "trapped" syndrome. The person who is feeling smothered can find *instant* relief if you, his partner, will implement the advice I have given. By making it clear that there are limits to what you can tolerate, you are showing self-respect and confidence. Strangely, that often draws the partner toward you. Some especially immature people absolutely *have* to feel there is a challenge in the relationship to be satisfied with it. Such individuals might even need to hear the door starting to close on the marriage before wanting to hustle back inside.

"Ridiculous!" you say. Of course it is. We only have one life to live so why spend it testing our loved ones and measuring the limits of their endurance? I don't know. But that's the way we are made. Why else will a toddler or a five-year-old or a teenager deliberately disobey his parents for no other reason than to determine how far Mom and Dad can be pushed? That same urge to test the limits causes students to harass teachers, employees to challenge bosses, privates to disobey sergeants, and so on. And regrettably, it leads some husbands and wives to test the ones they love, too. What is required in each instance is *discipline* and *self-respect* by the one on trial.

Now that I've presented the rationale for a period of confrontation in reponse to infidelity or other instances of blatant disrespect, I must hasten to explain what I mean by a crisis. I mentioned the possibility that Linda might separate from Paul to emphasize the seriousness of their situation. That is one way to heat things up, certainly, but moving out is not a step to take lightly. It may be the only method of getting a person's attention, but that is a decision requiring great individual wisdom and caution and prayer. The crisis of which I speak may or may not involve separation, but definitely encompasses much more.

The precipitated crisis, first, must be accompanied by an entire change of attitude. Instead of begging, pleading, wringing your hands and whimpering like an abused puppy, you as the vulnerable partner must appear strangely calm and assured. The key word is *confidence,* and it is of maximum importance. Your manner should say, "I believe in me. I'm no longer afraid. I can cope, regardless of the outcome. I know something I'm not talking about. I've had my day of sorrow and I'm through crying. God and I can handle whatever life puts in the path."

Not that you should say these things with words, of course.

In fact, the less said about your frame of mind, the better. It's your private business. One of the great errors made by the vulnerable lover when things begin to deteriorate is to talk too much. His secure partner is noncommunicative, evasive, deceptive and mysterious. He will not sit down and explain his inner feelings to the one who desperately needs that information. Remember the words of Nancy in her letter: "I long to get inside [my husband's] head and find out how he feels, but he simply won't talk about personal things." That is typical.

I'm recommending that you, the one who has sought to hold the marriage together, now choose your words more carefully, too. It is as though you and your mate have been involved in a table game with him hiding his cards and you permitting yours to be seen. This has given the independent partner more information than he should have had, especially about the pain you are experiencing. It is time to be more discreet. No more should you reveal your every thought and plan. *Under no circumstances should this book be shared or discussed.* And certainly, never make such statements as "I cried all night last night, Mindy. Oh, can't you see how much I need you!" *Crunch* goes the sound of the cage door coming back down. *Crack* goes the sound of respect starting to splinter again. *Slam* goes the sound of the door on Mindy's way out.

It is also important during this time of crisis not to do the predictable things. Having lived with you for years, your partner has you analyzed to a tee. He knows what bugs you, what makes you laugh, and what makes you cry. He has memorized all your little "pre-recorded" phrases that sprinkle your conversation. My advice is that you change these tapes. Don't offer him suggestions when you would typically do so. Don't make those inane remarks he's heard for twenty years. Don't be so predictable! Your purpose, you see, is to convince this man or woman that events are swirling out of control and may take him in directions he has not anticipated. The old rules don't apply. And why is this new mystery advantageous? Because one of the reasons your lover has lost interest in the relationship is that the "challenge" is gone. It's become so monotonous and routine. Hence, you would be wise to turn the whole thing upside down.

And by all means, unless there is business to be conducted, don't telephone a spouse who has separated. But if a call is necessary, state your reason for phoning after a few words of small talk and then get on with the matter at hand. When your business is finished, politely terminate the call and hang up. Do not, I repeat, do not get dragged into the usual verbal brawls. You don't want to appear to be an uptight crybaby merely covered by a thin veneer of poise. If you explode as you did in the past, it will be evident that you are, as he suspected, the weak old pushover he has come to disrespect. There may be a moment for anger if he insults you, but in that case keep your response crisp, controlled and confident.

An interesting thing happens when this kind of quiet confidence suddenly replaces the tears and self-pity of earlier days. Curiosity infects the aloof party and he begins to probe for details. For the first time in months, perhaps, he's coming your way. He's saying, "You seem different tonight," and, "I hope you're beginning to get over our problems." He's baiting you to find out what's going on inside. It is uncomfortable for him to observe that changes are occurring which he neither controls nor understands. Tell him nothing. He *needs* to wonder.

Throughout these changes, you must be careful not to behave in unloving ways. Remember that with God's help, you are attempting to build new bridges to this disrespectful, trapped partner. Don't burn them before they reach the other shore. Don't call him names, except to label his harmful behavior for what it is. Don't try to hurt him with gossip or even embarrassing truth. Don't telephone his family and try to undermine his position with them. Don't inflame hatred in the children of your union. And don't forget that your purpose is to be tough, yes, but loving as well.

Though it may be obvious, perhaps I should take just a moment to explain why these changes in manner and response are so necessary. Some may think I'm recommending silly little cat-and-mouse games to people who are engaged in life-and-death struggles. Isn't it a bit childish, they may say, to pretend to be confident when you're dying inside? Not so. These are the conclusions I've drawn from a lifetime of counseling experience.

The partner who is threatening to leave or chase another lover is rarely convinced beyond a shadow of a doubt that he's doing the right thing. He's equipped with a God-given conscience, after all, that is hammering him with guilt. You can be quite certain of that. He may appear resolute and determined, but we must assume that a tug of war is going on inside. He feels terrible about hurting his kids, for one thing. Furthermore, a spark of love may exist for you as the woman of his youth, glowing somewhere beneath his cold exterior. While his manner is saying, "I don't care anymore," he may be engaged in these kinds of secret conversations in his mind: "Have I hurt the best friend I ever had? Maybe I should call off this whole affair. But I sure don't want my relationship with Sue to go back to what it used to be. I *do* think I could love her again." Round and round go the pros and cons.

We can assume that some degree of self-doubt exists in a majority of husbands and wives who are threatening to leave. It certainly appears to be characteristic of Linda's husband, Paul (see p. 15). He just can't decide which woman he wants. We know, therefore, that Linda is still in the running, and that's good news. But how can she protect and encourage the tiny spark that smolders in his heart? Clearly, she must not smother it! She should give it plenty of room to breathe, hoping it will grow into a small flame. That is accomplished by calling off the offensive. Instead of pressuring Paul to act a certain way and to come home, Linda needs to make him wonder if he could *get her back.* Freedom, you see, is the fuel of romantic fire!

Now we come to the most important part of the crisis experience. I'm referring to a face-to-face encounter which must certainly occur soon. In fact, there will be several critical exchanges when you will be called upon to state your case. Don't blunder into those conversations unprepared. Carefully organize your thoughts and rehearse what you plan to convey. Talk this over with your counselor-advisor, seeking his perspectives on the issues. The central theme of the encounter should not focus on what you hope your partner will do, but on your own conclusions. If I were Linda, for example, I would say something like this:

It's a curious thing, Paul, how a person loses all perspective when he's so close to a problem. It becomes difficult to see the issues clearly, and that has definitely happened to me in recent months. But in the past few weeks I've been able to pull back from our difficulties and I now see everything in an entirely new light. It is incredible just how foolish I have been since you decided to leave. I have tolerated your unfaithfulness for almost a year, and was even so naïve as to permit Susan to come into our bedroom. I can't believe now that I did that. I guess I just loved you so much that I was willing to do anything you demanded, just to keep you from leaving me.

But I'll tell you, Paul, those days are over! If you want to go, you can certainly do so. In fact, that may be for the best. I doubt if I can ever trust you again or feel for you as I once did. I wasn't a perfect wife, to be sure, but no other man has touched me since I pledged myself to you. But you violated my trust—not once but repeatedly for all these months. I'm no longer special to you— I'm just one of a crowd. I can't live with that. I'd rather face life alone than as a member of your harem. If Susan is the one you want, I hope the two of you will be happy together. I'm still not sure how something so wonderful became so dirty and distorted, but that is between you and the Lord. We both have to answer to Him in our own way, and my conscience is clear.

So where do we go from here, Paul? I've been doing some intensive thinking, and believe you should pack up and leave. It just won't work for you to hopscotch between Susan and me, sleeping with us both and trying to make it all seem so normal. You say you aren't sure which one you want? Well, that isn't very inspiring to me. You pledged eternal love and commitment to me on our wedding day, but now that could be gone with the toss of a coin. What we both need is some time apart. I think you should find another place to stay, perhaps with Susan if you wish. If in the future you decide you want to be my husband, then we'll talk about it. I make no promises, however. I'm doing everything possible to remove you from my heart, to spare myself any more pain. It's not going to be easy. You were my only love—the only one I ever wanted. But that was then and this is now. God bless you, Paul. The kids and I will miss you.

Can there be any doubt that Paul would be shocked by this candid approach? For over a year, he's been trying to get this nagging woman off his back. She has called him on the phone and begged him to come over—and inevitably, ended each conversation in tears. He has done everything to escape from Linda's cage, including insulting her, making ridiculous sexual demands and threatening a divorce. But nothing has worked. He wonders, "How in the world can the ol' lady keep her self-respect? I treat her like a dog and she just keeps coming back!" Linda is obviously desperate.

Then, without warning, her entire demeanor begins to change. The next time they are together, Linda seems more confident, more in control. She asks for nothing and even appears rather bored with the conversation. "What's going on?" Paul wonders. "Has she found another man? Is some dude moving in on my territory? Is he going to be sleeping in my bed and expecting my kids to call him dad? Hold on a minute! Am I about to lose something very important to me?"

Two weeks later, Linda delivers the speech I suggested. She feels uncomfortable trying to say it face to face, so she sits down and expresses her thoughts in writing. (This is recommended since words can be chosen more carefully without counter arguments and interruptions; also, a letter becomes a permanent document to be read and reread in the days ahead.)

Paul finds the envelope in his mailbox that evening when

he gets home from work. "Here we go again," he sighs. "I'll bet Linda is begging me not to see Susan anymore." Instead, she has granted him freedom to leave and even urged him to do so. His cage door springs open and his wife suddenly takes on an aura of self-respect and dignity. For a certain percentage of people like Linda and Paul, that is the beginning of the healing process.

# 8.

# *Three Women Who Tried It*

*I* wish that it might be possible for you, the reader, to get behind my eyes and perceive our subject as I see it. If only you could know intimately the brokenhearted husbands and wives I have counseled who floundered on a policy of appeasement and panic, and then with God's help, discovered the principles of self-respect and romantic freedom. But more important, I wish I could convey the broader applicability of these concepts to those with healthy marriages, to dating teenagers and unmarried adults, to employers and parents and governments. *Respect,* the critical ingredient in human affairs, is generated by quiet dignity, self-confidence and common courtesy. It is assassinated by hand wringing, groveling in the dirt, and pleas for mercy.

Given the limitations of language in attempting to convey these concepts, it seems advantageous to let my friends tell their own stories. In this chapter are letters from three women who have been where Roger, Linda, Faye and Nancy are today.* They wrote to me in response to a series of radio programs devoted to the topic of this book. I think you will find their experience to be inspirational and enlightening.

We'll begin with an anonymous letter from a very intelligent lady who knows the meaning of pain.

---

* Roger's letter appears on pp. 11–12; Linda's, pp. 14–15; Faye's, pp. 22–23; and Nancy's, pp. 32–33.

Dear Dr. Dobson:

After listening to your radio series, "Love Must Be Tough," I would like to tell you my own story. It is difficult to discuss the facts, even today, because my husband was a prominent minister serving a large congregation before he fell into sin.

It all started when a man from our church appeared at my front door, asking if he could talk to me. He brought with him a letter which proved unmistakably that my husband was involved with another woman. I never dreamed that anything was going on and my shock was overwhelming. The man told me the full details, and after leaving, proceeded to tell the rest of the world. He reproduced the documents and circulated them throughout our church and all over town.

Dr. Dobson, never in my life have I felt so all alone as when this affair became public knowledge. I was treated like a "leper" by members of our congregation. My husband was immediately forced to resign, requiring us to move out of the parsonage. Suddenly, we had no home, no job, no money, and *very* few friends. We had given our lives to helping other people, but no one was there when we were down. I can't describe the anger and scorn that was hurled at us. We were subjected to physical threats, harassment by mail and by phone, damage to our property, incredible gossip and false accusations. It was an awful time of our lives.

Not only had I lost everything overnight, but my marriage was about gone, too. Before moving, I went into my bedroom and fell on my face before God, asking Him to take over. He was the only one I could talk to. A person simply does not discuss such matters with those who don't understand. Finally, the Lord directed me to a wise counselor who sat and listened to my story. I told him of my great guilt for the role I played in our problems and how terrible I felt. I'll never forget his reply.

He told me not to take the blame for my husband's affair, and that nothing I had done could justify his infidelity. He advised me to stand up and be firm with him, even though it would be difficult. It was, he said, the only way to save our marriage. We agreed that divorce was not the answer, even though I had scriptural grounds to leave him. I decided to pay the price to confront my husband.

A few months later the crisis came. I gave Milan an ultimatum—either go with the other woman or stay with me. He could not have both of us any longer. I put my hands on his shoulders and looked him straight in the eye and said, "You know you are to blame for what has happened to us. You committed adultery, I didn't." I told him if he loved the other woman more than me, then he should leave. I would accept it. I reminded him that he had a soul and would someday answer to God.

Milan not only broke off the affair, but he later thanked me for having the courage to stick it out with him through this difficult time. It was not easy but we worked it out and our family survived.

Since then, God has blessed us tremendously. The Lord helped me forgive Milan, reminding me that He had also forgiven so many of my sins. We are now back in the ministry in Oregon, and my husband is more effective for God than he has ever been. Our three children have adjusted well. I shielded them from hate for the church or disrespect for their father. They love their dad so much.

Yes, Dr. Dobson, *"Love must be tough!"* Had I given up and taken the easy way out, our story would not have had such a happy ending. It took hard work, struggle and prayer, but the Lord put our home back together. At first I thought I would never be able to smile again, but He has removed the clouds and brought us sunshine once more.

I know it isn't proper not to sign one's name, but under the circumstances, I feel it is better to remain anonymous. I would love to meet you and Shirley, sometime.

Isn't that an inspirational letter? It should be obvious why I wanted to share it in this context. Unfortunately, adultery among the clergy is becoming increasingly common. Ministers are usually busy men in high-pressure positions that limit the amount of time they can spend with their families. When that strain at home is combined with the natural access ministers have to admiring women, the temptations for indiscretion are apparent. The same condition prevails in my profession, as well. One study revealed that 25 percent of female students in secular schools of psychology have slept with their major professors during their graduate training. What an incredible commentary that is on the moral state of the so-called "helping sciences"! Let's turn now to another letter that came in response to the same series of broadcasts. It is representative of hundreds that were received.

Dear Dr. Dobson:

I listened to your radio program last week and was so glad to hear you tell a person how to handle adultery by a spouse. I went through this during the past two years. My first counselor told me to be kind, loving, etc., and to win him back by my pleasantness. It didn't work. Things got worse until I couldn't stand it anymore.

That's when I went to another counselor and also sought the advice of my pastor. They both advised me to be strong, as you suggested. It was so different and seemed unscriptural, yet the Lord used them to teach me how to cope with the situation. Gradually, I felt better about myself and my self-respect returned. Then the Lord brought my husband back. It has been almost a year now since we started over and things are going well.

I want to encourage you to keep up the advice that *love must be tough*. It is hard to let go—especially when you are so confused and hurt. But it was only when I did turn loose that the Lord worked more in my husband's life.

If you ever print that series of messages, send me a copy please.

In Christ,
Lonna

Admittedly, these letters sound like phony Cinderella stories designed to support my particular biases. However, they represent real letters on file from living, breathing people who exist somewhere out there in the American culture. (I have changed some of the details to conceal the identities of the writers and to eliminate irrelevant comments.) The majority of the responses I received to the *Love Must Be Tough* broadcasts were like the ones I have shared—strong testimonials for the advice I've offered. Not every marriage was saved, of course. I am certainly no magician and the application of toughness does not remove the free will of a wayward spouse. But even when divorce was reported by those who wrote, the advantages of quiet self-respect as opposed to unbridled panic were usually apparent.

Finally, let's look at a letter from a woman who saw *herself* in the examples I gave. Her husband is holding her by force and she is disrespecting him in return. I found this response interesting from one who represents the other side of the coin.

Dear Friend,

I listened in amazement to your radio program, "Love Must Be Tough," and saw my own marriage in your discussion. I have known it was troubled but didn't understand why. Now it is clear.

You see, I have had many of the disrespectful attitudes toward my husband that you described (did you read my mind?). I have been embarrassed by him in public because he is not a good conversationalist and because he seems so dumb (although he is not). I was actually ashamed to be with him!

On the other hand, you described my husband correctly, too. He has had a stranglehold of control over me, resenting any friendships or commitments I've had outside the home.

I can see now that we were responding to each other's attitudes without a word being spoken about either. I was feeling stifled and he was feeling rejected.

Although I have not sought an extramarital affair, I can see now that I have been a prime candidate for one. I don't want that for myself or my family! Mixed in with my feelings is the low self-esteem you talked about, too.

We have a Christian counseling center here in St. Louis which I have consulted in the past. A counselor there told me some of the same things you said on the radio, but I was not ready to hear them. Now I am. I believe God used your comments to open my eyes to our problems so that He can heal them.

I thank God for the power and strength of your ministry and the way He is using it to speak to my needs. Facing oneself is not easy, but the growth that results is exciting. How many times that old adage, "Ignorance is bliss," has been shown to be so much nonsense in my life.

Love,
Charlotte

For all those readers who could not write positive and hopeful letters like those I've shared, I trust that God will use these pages to encourage you and begin the healing process. The Lord is, after all, in the business of performing miracles.

# 9.

# *Questions and Answers*

*I*t is never possible to cover all aspects of a topic so complex as the emotional interplay between human beings. Something important is certain to be left out of the text. In those instances, I have found it useful to toss in a section devoted to questions and answers. That permits me to gather up loose ends and elaborate on areas of confusion.

The following questions are obviously written for this purpose, therefore, but they represent actual inquiries I've heard from hundreds of people with a need to know.

Q. My wife has been involved in an affair with her boss for six months. I've known about it from the beginning but just haven't been able to confront her. Melanie acts like she doesn't love me anyway. If I give her an ultimatum I could lose her completely. Can you assure me that that won't happen? Have you ever offered the *love must be tough* advice and had it backfire, ending in divorce?

A. Yes, I have, and I certainly understand your caution. I wish I could guarantee how Melanie will react to a firmer approach. Unfortunately, life offers few certainties, even when all the probabilities point in one direction. Sometimes well-conditioned athletes drop dead from heart attacks. Some outstanding parents raise children who rebel and become drug addicts. Some of the most intelligent, cautious business-men foolishly bankrupt themselves. Life is like that. Things happen every day that shouldn't have occurred. Neverthe-less, we should go with the best information available to us. I read a sign on a wall this week that said, "The fastest horses don't always win, but you should still bet on them." Even as a nongambler, that makes sense to me.

Having offered that explanation, let me say that there is nothing risky about treating oneself with greater respect, exhibiting confidence and poise, pulling backward and re-leasing the door on the romantic trap. The positive benefits of that approach are often immediate and dramatic. Loving self-respect virtually never fails to have a salutary effect on a drifting lover, unless there is not the tiniest spark left to fan. Thus, in instances when opening the cage door results in a spouse's sudden departure, *the relationship was in the coffin, already.* I'm reminded of the old proverb that says, "If you love something, set it free. If it comes back to you, it's yours. If it doesn't come back, it never was yours in the first place." There is great truth in that adage, and it applies to your relationship with your wife.

Now, obviously, it *is* risky to precipitate a period of crisis. When explosive individuals are involved in mid-life turmoil or a passionate fling with a new lover, great tact and wisdom are required to know when and how to respond. That's why Christian professional counsel is vital before, during and after the confrontation. It would be unthinkable of me to recommend that victims of affairs indiscriminately pose ultimatums with 24-hour deadlines, or that they push an independent partner into a corner. Great caution is needed in such delicate conflicts, and certainly, no move should be made without much prayer and supplication before the Lord.

In short, I suggest that you seek the assistance of a compe-tent counselor who can help you deal with the problem of Melanie's affair.

**Q.** If you were the counselor who was helping someone manage a crisis situation like the one described above, you would obviously be making recommendations that could kill the marriage. Doesn't that make you nervous? Have you ever regretted taking a family in this direction?

**A.** To answer that question you need to understand how I see my situation. My role is similar to that of a surgeon who tells a patient that he needs a coronary artery by-pass operation. The man sits in his doctor's office, hearing the probabilities of success and failure. "If you undergo this operation," the doctor says, "you'll have—we'll say—a three percent chance of not surviving the surgery." Wow! three out of every hundred people who submit to the knife will die on the table! Why would anyone run that risk voluntarily? Because the chances of death are far greater without the surgery.

The *love must be tough* confrontations and ultimatum are like that. They may result in the sudden demise of a relationship. But, without the crisis, there is a much higher probability of a lingering death. Instead of bringing the matter to a head while there is a chance for healing, the alternative is to stand by while the marriage dies with a whimper. I'd rather take my chances today, before further damage is done. As I said, a blowout is better than a slow leak.

**Q.** My marriage seems beyond repair to me. My husband is just like Linda's; he's running around with other women and threatening to divorce me. Is there really any hope for us?

**A.** It's difficult to say without knowing the details, but I can tell you this. I've seen dozens of families who were in your fix but are now happy and whole. I taught a Sunday School class for young married couples for a number of years, and right there under my nose in a conservative church, infidelity was a surprisingly common event. There was one period of time during which I dealt with nineteen different couples where extramarital affairs had either occurred or were seriously threatening. These families are still known to me, and nine of them are apparently happily married today. Though this percentage may seem low, remember that these were families on the verge of divorce that have now survived ten years or longer. Loving toughness played a role in their recovery, although their commitment to the Christian faith was *the* significant factor. So yes, hope springs eternal, as well it should.

Let me give you one final word of encouragement. Nothing can seem so fixed but change so rapidly as human emotions. When it comes to romantic endeavors, feelings can turn upside down in a day or two. I've seen husbands or wives who expressed hatred for their spouses, saying, "I never want to see you again," only to fall weeping in the other person's arms some hours later.

Hang tough. God isn't through with you and your husband yet.

**Q.** You've referred to the case of Linda and Paul repeatedly throughout the book. Tell me what you would recommend to her if Paul came back asking her to forgive him and take him back. Should she just throw her arms open and pretend the affair never happened?

**A.** Well, she should certainly take him back. That's the point of everything I've written. But her power to negotiate needed changes will never be greater than in that moment, and she should not deal it away too quickly. I would suggest that she get Paul's written commitment to participate in counseling *immediately,* not even waiting two or three weeks to get started. Old patterns will persist if serious effort is not made to change them. This family also has some deep wounds to work through and they're not likely to complete that healing process on their own. Linda must make it clear that *never* again—and I mean *never*—will she tolerate sexual unfaithfulness. Paul needs this motivation to go straight. He must know, and *believe,* that one more romp with another lover and the sky will surely fall. Linda must convince him that she means business. If he wavers, even slightly, she should give him another month or two to sit somewhere wishing he could come home. Better that they continue at the door of matrimonial death now than to go through the misery of infidelity again in a few years. Finally, Linda should insist on some major spiritual commitments within the family. This couple is going to need the healing powers of God and His grace if they are to rebuild what sin has eroded.

Then when Linda gets Paul home again, she should work like never before to make the man happy.

Q. How difficult is it for people to implement the advice you are offering? I'm referring to the wounded and broken person who sees everything slipping away. Isn't it really tough for that man or woman to square up his or her shoulders and face the possibility of losing the one he/she loves?

A. Sure, it's hard. Some people have told me flatly that they couldn't do it. Others never quite comprehend what I've said. But to those who make even a small step in the direction of confidence, the rewards are instantaneous. For the person who has cried for days and lost a lot of weight and chewed the fingernails off both hands, you can't imagine what a relief it is to gain some self-respect again. Then when his partner also shows a measure of respect for the first time in months, the effect is exhilarating. As a bystander, I love it too!

Q. Several months ago my husband announced that he was divorcing me for another woman. Since then he has been seeing her regularly but he hasn't left home and seems to be in a state of confusion. He's lost fifteen pounds and just looks terrible. What do you think is going on in his mind? He won't talk to me about his feelings and he becomes angry when I ask him questions.

A. It is likely that your husband is experiencing intense guilt and conflict that often accompanies a selfish and sinful act such as infidelity. God has placed a little voice in the human soul that screams bloody murder at such moments, although some of us have learned to stuff a fist in its mouth. Even when we ignore its condemnation, the conscience is a formidable opponent of irresponsibility and it will not permit gross violations of moral laws without a struggle. It is not uncommon for a person in this situation to experience a kind of internal war that can only be resolved in one of three ways: (1) the conscience wins and the person returns to the straight life; (2) the person rationalizes so effectively that his behavior begins to seem pure and holy; or (3) the conscience wins but the person persists in doing what he wants to do anyway.

People in this third category, which may include your husband, can be some of the most miserable men and women on the face of the earth. Their behavior has contradicted their personal code of ethics and all attempts to reconcile the two have been futile. Stated another way, these individuals are in a dog fight with their consciences, and the fur is flying in all directions. Not only psychological disorders but physical illness can result from such disharmony! A person who is going through this internal conflict often experiences depression, weight loss, sleepless nights, nail biting, etc. The ordeal is extremely uncomfortable to the sensitive individual.

If we are right about your husband's frame of mind, you can expect him to commit himself very quickly either to you or the other woman. It is simply too painful to remain in suspended animation between good and evil. I would advise you to seek professional counsel as to whether this is the proper moment to require your husband to make his choice. With the few facts I've been given, I would lean in that direction.

Q. It has always been my understanding that marriage was supposed to be based on *unconditional* love. That is, the commitment to one another should be independent of behavior, no matter how offensive or unfaithful. But your concept of accountability in marriage seems to be saying, "I will love you as long as you do what I want."

A. You've misunderstood my point. The limitations of language make it very difficult to explain this concept adequately, but let me try again. I certainly believe in the validity of unconditional love, and in fact, the mutual accountability I have recommended is an expression of that love! For example, if a husband (or wife) is behaving in ways that will harm himself, his children, his marriage and the family of the "other woman," then confrontation with him becomes an act of love. The easiest response by the innocent partner would be to look the other way and pretend she doesn't notice. But from my perspective, that is tantamount to a parent's refusing to confront a fourteen-year-old who comes home drunk at 4:00 A.M. That mother or father has an obligation to create a crisis in response to destructive behavior. I'm trying to say that *unconditional love* is not synonymous with permissiveness, passivity and weakness. Sometimes it requires toughness and discipline and accountability.

Q. When my wife left me for another man, I felt like the whole thing was my fault. I still feel that way. I had never even looked at another woman, yet here I am taking the blame for her affair. Rationally, I know I'm very unfair to myself, but I can't help it. Or can I?

A. It is *the* typical reaction of a victim, like yourself, to take the full responsibility for the behavior of an unfaithful spouse. I dealt with this situation in a prior book and feel it might be helpful to quote from that source here:

It has always been surprising for me to observe how often the wounded marriage partner—the person who was clearly the victim of the other's irresponsibility—is the one who suffers the greatest pangs of guilt and feelings of inferiority. How strange that the one who tried to hold things together in the face of obvious rejection often finds herself wondering, "How did I fail him?— I just wasn't woman enough to hold my man . . . I am 'nothing' or he wouldn't have left . . . if only I had been more exciting as a sexual partner . . . I drove him to it . . . I wasn't pretty enough . . . I didn't deserve him in the first place."

The blame for marital disintegration is seldom the fault of the husband or wife alone. It takes two to tangle, as they say, and there is always some measure of shared blame for a divorce. However, when one marriage partner makes up his mind to behave irresponsibly, to become involved extramaritally, or to run from his family commitments and obligations, he usually seeks to justify his behavior by magnifying the failures of his spouse. "You didn't meet my needs, so I had to satisfy them somewhere else," is the familiar accusation. By increasing the guilt of his partner in this way, he reduces his own culpability. For a husband or wife with low self-esteem, these charges and recriminations are accepted as fact when hurled his way. "Yes, it was my fault. I drove you to it!" Thus, the victim assumes the full responsibility for his partner's irresponsibility, and self-worth shatters.

I would not recommend that you sit around hating the memory of your husband. Bitterness and resentment are emotional cancers that rot us from within. However, I would encourage you to examine the facts carefully. Answers to these questions should be sought: "Despite my human frailties, did I value my marriage and try to preserve it? Did my husband decide to destroy it and then seek justification for his actions? Was I given a fair chance to resolve the areas of greatest irritation? Could I have held him even if I had made all the changes he wanted? Is it reasonable that I should hate myself for this thing that has happened?"

You should know that social rejection breeds feelings of inferiority and self-pity in enormous proportions. And rejection by the one you love, particularly, is the most powerful destroyer of self-esteem in the entire realm of human experience. You might begin to see yourself as a victim of this process, rather than a worthless failure at the game of love.*

Q. My wife tried to make me feel guilty when she left. She angrily blamed me for the divorce despite my desperate

---

\* *Dr. Dobson Answers Your Questions* (Wheaton, IL: Tyndale House, 1982), pp. 306–7.

attempts to hold things together. In her mind, I failed so miserably as a husband that she was forced to run around with her boss! Are you saying that this transfer of responsibility is typical when one spouse has been unfaithful?

**A.** Yes, it often happens. Guilt is a very painful emotion, and the person who is willfully tearing up a home in pursuit of a new lover is in an uncomfortable position. He or she feels condemnation from four primary sources—from the rejected husband or wife, from the children, from friends and associates, and from God. In order to justify his behavior, he energetically constructs a verbal defense around those who would testify against him in a court of moral law. His purpose, of course, is to make adultery seem reasonable and downright godly. That takes some creativity!

Ask any victim of an affair; he or she has probably heard a specialized version of the following rationalizations:

1. To resolve marital guilt . . . "I know that what I'm doing is difficult for you now, but someday you will understand that it is for the best. I never really loved you even when we were young. In fact, we should never have gotten married in the first place. Furthermore, this divorce is really *your* fault. You drove me to it by————[insert grievances here, such as frigidity, in-law problems, nagging, overwork, or all the foregoing].

This message has a transparent purpose. The first sentence marvelously purifies the motives of the unfaithful spouse. It says in effect, "I'm really doing this for your good." The second sentence is also a beauty. It is designed to serve as an "annulment" to the marriage instead of a cruel abandonment of a loved one. By saying that they should never have gotten married, their union becomes an unfortunate mistake rather than a relationship which God Himself ordained and cemented. (Henry VIII used this approach to eject his first wife, Catherine of Aragon.) Then by putting the remaining responsibility on the other party, what was left of the blame is successfully transferred from the guilty to the innocent. So much for wedding vows. Now let's deal with the children.

2. To resolve parental guilt . . . "This will be hard on the kids for a while, but they'll be better off in the long run. It certainly isn't healthy for them to see us fight and argue like we've been doing. Besides, I will spend just as much time with them after things settle down as I do now."

Zap! Zap! Guilt over the children is also tucked away. Would you believe that Dad's escapade with another woman or Mom's flight with Don Juan is actually a constructive thing? Never mind what the children see and comprehend with their big, beautiful eyes. Pay no heed to the conclusions they draw about why Mommy or Daddy left, and why he or she doesn't love them anymore, and why God let it happen, and why the divorce may have been *their* fault, and why life is so painful and scary. Try to ignore the fact that everything stable has just come unstitched in the lives of some very impressionable and sensitive kids. Don't think about it, and maybe your rapidly beating heart will return to normal again. Guilt over the children can be the toughest to rationalize, but, fortunately, hundreds of books and tapes are available today that will help you silence your writhing conscience.

3. To resolve social guilt . . . "I'm sure our friends won't understand at first and I can hardly wait to hear what your mother will have to say. But it's like I told the pastor last week, our divorce is really no one's fault. We've just outgrown each other. People change as the years go by, and relationships have to change to accommodate them." (If a woman is speaking she may say: "Besides, I am entitled to do what's best for *me* once

in a while. I've given my entire life to everyone else—now it's time for me to think of myself. It's only fair that I fit into the picture at some point, and this is it. Anyway, what's right for me will prove best for you and the children, too.")

This line of reasoning has been provided for women today almost word for word by the more radical elements of the feminist movement. It is only one of many rationalizations by which selfishness can be purified and made to appear altruistic. Three down and one to go.

4. To resolve divine guilt . . . "I've prayed about this decision and I am now certain that God approves of what I've chosen to do."

There it is, folks, in living color—the ultimate rationalization. If the Creator in His infinite wisdom has taken the matter under advisement and judged the divorce to be in the best interest of everyone, who can argue that point further? The conversation is over. Sin has been sanctified. Guilt is expunged. Self-respect is restored . . . and, alas, evil has prevailed. Having settled the "big four," every moral and spiritual obstacle is removed. The stage is set for separation and/or divorce.

**Q.** I know now that my husband is a "womanizer"—a guy who can't resist anything in a skirt. Will he always be like this? Can I change him?

**A.** It is difficult, if not impossible, to change anyone. It certainly cannot be accomplished by nagging and complaining and chastising. That only causes a person to dig in his heels and fight to the finish. What you can do is what I've suggested in this book: make it clear to your husband that he can't have you and a harem too, and that he must make a choice between his lust and his love. Unfortunately, merely putting these alternatives before him verbally will not force him to select one over the other. He would rather have *both* toys. That's why there will probably come a time for *loving toughness* when you back your words by firmness and definitive action. Remember in that difficult hour that God *can* change your husband, and that the crisis may be a divine vehicle to bring him to his senses.

**Q.** You implied earlier that the *love must be tough* philosophy has broad applicability. I understand its role in reconstructing a bad marriage. How would it function in a good relationship?

**A.** The best way of keeping a marriage healthy is to maintain a system of mutual accountability, within the context of love. Speaking personally, the secret of my beautiful relationship with Shirley for the past twenty-three years has involved a careful protection of the "line of respect" between us. This is a difficult concept to convey and its function is different from one personality to another. Perhaps by explaining how it operates between Shirley and me, I can help the reader adapt the principle to his own circumstances.

Suppose I work in my office two hours longer than usual on a particular night, knowing Shirley is preparing a special candlelight dinner. The phone sits there on my desk, but I lack the concern to make a brief call to explain. As the evening wears on, Shirley wraps the cold food in foil and puts it in the refrigerator. Then suppose when I finally get home, I do not apologize. Instead, I sit down with a newspaper and abruptly tell Shirley to get my dinner ready. You can bet there'll be a few minutes of fireworks in the Dobson household. Shirley will rightfully interpret my behavior as insulting and will move to defend the "line of respect" between us. We will talk it out and next time I'll be more considerate.

Let's put the shoe on the other foot. Suppose Shirley knows I need the car at 2:00 P.M. for some important purpose, but she deliberately keeps me waiting. Perhaps she sits in a restaurant with a lady friend, drinking coffee and talking. Meanwhile, I'm pacing the floor at home wondering where she is. It is very likely that my lovely wife will hear about my dissatisfaction when she gets home. The "line of respect" has been violated, even though the offense was minor.

This is what I mean by mutual accountability. Such minor conflict in a marriage plays a positive role in establishing what is and is not acceptable behavior. Some instances of disrespect are petty, like the two examples I gave, but when they are permitted to pass unnoticed, two things happen. First, the offender is unaware that he has stepped over the line and is likely to repeat the indiscretion later. In fact, he may go farther into the other person's territory the next time. Second, the person who felt insulted then internalizes the small irritation rather than spilling it out. As the interpretation of disrespect grows and the corresponding agitation accumulates in a storage tank, the stage is set for an eventual explosion, rather than a series of minor ventilations.

What I'm saying is that some things are worth fighting over, and at the top of the list is the "line of respect." Most of my conflicts with Shirley have occurred over some behavior that one of us interpreted as unhealthy to the relationship. Shirley may say to me, in effect, "Jim, what you did was selfish and I can't let it pass." She is careful not to insult me in the confrontation, keeping her criticism focused on the behavior to which she objected.

A workable system of checks and balances of this nature helps a couple keep their marriage on course for a marathon rather than a sprint. And I can assure you, Shirley and I are going for the distance!

Q. That philosophy contradicts what I have been taught by Christian leaders who say as believers, "We have no rights." If I understand what they say, I should not even notice instances of disrespect because I have no rights to be defended. Do you disagree?

A. Perhaps. That "no rights" philosophy would be unbeatable

if both partners were totally mature, unselfish and loving. Unfortunately, we are all riddled with imperfection and self-serving desires. Therefore, we *need* reinforcement and accountability in order to do what is right. When only one member of the family buys the "no rights" concept and tries to implement it, a marriage can be blown apart. Why? Because the nonparticipating spouse begins to crawl all over the "line of respect." He gets the lion's share of everything—money, sex, power, fun and games, etc. Knowing the partner's spiritual obligation, he feels entitled by divine decree to do as he pleases.

The Christian spouse who is clinging desperately to this theological understanding is not made of steel. Nor is he blind. He sees instance after instance of disrespect, and does his best to ignore them. But they go straight into a memory bank, whether he wishes to store them or not. That's the way he's made. Then one day when his resistance is down, perhaps when he is exhausted, or in a woman's case, during the pressures of premenstrual tension, a hydrogen bomb can be detonated that may blow off the head of her startled husband. A "no rights" position would have carried that person through a short race; unfortunately, life is so *daily,* and the runner weakened on heartbreak hill.

I must hasten to offer an important disclaimer. *Any* recommendation can be carried to extremes, including defense of the "line of respect." There are millions of women, especially, who need nothing less than an excuse to harangue their spouses over perceived violations of one sort or another. They do that better than anything else in life. Their poor husbands live with a constant barrage of complaints and criticisms, knowing they can do *nothing* right. Then here comes Dobson advising, "Hold 'em accountable, ladies!"

That's not what I intended to say. Remember that 1 Corinthians 13:5 tells us "love is not easily provoked." That tolerance is certainly evident in good marriages. Husbands and wives must overlook a multitude of flaws in one another and not howl over the speck in a partner's eye when the accuser has a log sticking out of his own. Prolonged anger can kill a marriage—especially when it reflects perceived wrongs from the past that have never been forgiven.

Thus, the *love must be tough* concept does not suggest that people become touchy and picky; it *does* hold that genuine instances of disrespect should be acknowledged and handled within the context of love. And certainly, when major violations occur that threaten the relationship, such as Linda's husband running to see a sexy divorcee night after night, they should be met head-on. By confronting him when he got home she would not have been fighting for her "rights," at all; she would have been defending her marriage! We've seen what happens when that defense is lacking.

**Q.** To be certain that I understand what you mean by the "line of respect" principle, could you discuss it further? Do you deal with this idea often in your marriage counseling?

**A.** In virtually every troubled family I see, the "line of respect" has crumbled. Sometimes the wife is trampling on the husband's territory; sometimes he is all over hers. Either way, within five minutes in my office it is apparent that there is an absence of fair play by one of two partners. Here's an extreme example as described in a letter from a woman whose line is now in shambles.

"My husband and I have three children and I am with them day and night because I can't drive. My husband doesn't want me to go anywhere, anyway. He is very domineering. He dishes out the money and decides how every dollar will be spent.

This past week was terrible. Mike wouldn't let the kids sing or talk in the car. He orders all of us to bed at a certain time and controls all TV and radio stations. I like to hear you on Christian radio but he won't let me listen when he's home. He will change stations and then go downstairs. I sometimes tape your program secretly and play it after Mike is gone. Mike's grand-mother lives with us too and she thinks he is being mean to the whole family.

I would never get to go anywhere if it wasn't for good neighbors who take me to church functions. I just feel like I have no freedom at all and my nerves are beginning to act up. The kids are afraid of Mike too.

Anything you can do to help me would be *greatly* appreciated."

Fortunately, most cases are not as devoid of respect as this one, but it illustrates the problem. If I were working with this woman, my objective would be to teach her how to hold her own with her husband without blowing her mar-riage off the face of the earth. It would be a delicate task.

Q. I have a male physician friend who can't seem to resist the charms of his female patients. His marriage is in serious difficulty even though I know he loves his wife. Would you explain the psychological dynamics in this kind of prob-lem, and tell me what I should say to help my friend?

A. A similar question was addressed recently in an issue of the *Christian Medical Society Journal* where reference was made to an excellent article by Dr. Merville Vincent entitled "The Physician's Own Well-Being."* Dr. Vincent discussed twelve hazardous assumptions that can ruin a physician's career. One of those assumptions, quoted below, is the belief by the male doctor that he is God's gift to women.

Some patients fall in love with their doctor. The scenario often goes something like this. The patient is a young lady with a minor illness and is unhappily married or divorced. She comes to her physician not only with her specific complaints, but at a time when she is feeling frightened and helpless. In his office, the doctor seems strong, confident, calm and caring. He knows what to do and does it. He helps her with her presenting problem. She then is relieved and gains strength from his confidence. She begins

---

* Vincent, M. O., "The Physician's Own Well-Being," *Annals Royal College of Physicians and Surgeons of Canada 1981*, vol. 14, 4, 277–81.

to think, "Isn't he wonderful, he'd be so nice to have around the house." Meanwhile, back in the doctor's home, his wife is also thinking, "He'd be so nice to have around the house" or less kindly, "If patients could only see him like I do."

Next our patient communicates to the doctor that he's wonderful. He immediately agrees and, after careful thought, concludes that she is a genius and wishes his wife was smart this way also. He says to himself "excellent judge of men, that girl."

The problem is he mistakes her needs for his assets. Typically, the situation involves two people with unmet needs. The physician at risk is one whose needs to be cared for are not being met at home. Sometimes this has been due to his business; sometimes because he denied any such needs. Often his wife is tired of giving of herself with little apparent attempt by her husband to meet her various needs for a husband and father of her children. She is now putting demands on her husband to do something at home. She is tired of feeling she is nothing but his housekeeper and sexual partner. He often responds to these demands by feeling unappreciated and nothing but the breadwinner. At such a time, he is a sitting duck for a relationship with a young lady with needs that also make her vulnerable. The affair at first not only boosts sagging self-esteem for both, but seems to offer the doctor a relationship in which he may receive much more admiration than he gets at home and with much less responsibility. She, who has no right to this man, can be warm and accepting at first. Meanwhile, his wife, who feels she has a right to him, is becoming more angry and frustrated about his absence from the house. Later the young lady begins to feel jealous. Now our emotionally and physically depleted doctor feels he has two demanding women and still no one to look after him.

How may such a predicament be prevented? First, realize it happens, and it starts primarily because of the role of the two people in the situation. Realize it begins because of her needs, not your assets. Realize that when you meet dependent needs with an erotic response, you become part of the problem, not part of the solution. The best prevention is to be sure that your own needs to be cared for (dependent needs) are being met. These are best met in a marriage where there is reciprocity of mutual need-meeting. Perhaps the early warning signal is when you begin to feel that your patients appreciate you and love you more than your wife and family do. The next step may be to spend even more time with patients and less with your spouse.

Q. My husband is a very attractive man and he's the president of his own company at a young age. I know that women are out to get him, especially some divorced secretaries who constantly flirt with him. I'm raising these kids here at home and I have to admit that I worry about holding Dwight. I believe he's been faithful to me, but I wonder if he will always turn down the opportunities around him? I mean, he comes home and tells me what these women do and say, and I can't believe it! They practically proposition him. What can I do to hang onto my husband?

A. Twenty years ago, your question would have seemed unnecessarily anxious and even a bit silly. But it makes plenty of sense today—the world has changed that much. There has always been hanky-panky going on, but never has it been so blatant and never have males and females been so bold in their pursuit of one another. More to the point of your concern, it is no longer considered taboo for an available woman to consciously lure a married man—even one with several children at home. He's fair game to anyone who can entice him away from his family. A woman told me recently that her nice-looking husband reports that girls deliberately brush against him in the subway and make risqué comments. Men are just as audacious in their pursuit of women, whether those women are married or not. Thus, the concern expressed in your question has a basis in reality.

Nevertheless, the solution is *not* to "hang onto" Dwight. You must not build a cage around him in an attempt to reduce your anxieties. That would only add unnecessary stresses to your relationship. Dwight must stay with you of his own free will—the same reason for which he married you in the first place. *Love must be free,* even in a world of sexual intrigue and disloyalty.

Perhaps it would be helpful for me to offer a couple of perspectives that may not have occurred to you. First, Dwight is primarily responsible for the insecurity you feel, one way or the other. He could allay your fears if he wished. It's a fairly simple task for a man to let his wife know he is committed to her for life. Instead, Dwight is regularly telling you about the sexy women who hang onto him and beg for his favors. *That's* the source of your butterflies. Indeed, most instances of "competition anxiety" among homemakers can be attributed to husbands like Dwight who subtly create insecurities in their wives.

Why would a man do such a thing? What can be gained by dangling a partner in suspense over something so basic as a marital commitment? Well, the male ego enjoys being desired by women—lots of women. That's why a married man will flirt with female employees even when he has no intention of being unfaithful. Furthermore, he will tell his wife about these admirers in order to gain "power" in their relationship. Whether consciously or not, he is saying by these disclosures, "You'd better treat me right because there are plenty of other women out there just waiting to get their hands on me."

At some point in your conversation with Dwight, these dynamics should be discussed. I'm not suggesting that you hammer him with accusations or complaints, but an opportunity may come to verbalize your feelings and put the matter of competition in proper perspective. The healthiest families are those that can discuss this kind of sensitive subject in an atmosphere of openness and acceptance.

Before that conversation ensues, however, I think you should look at a related issue. The way you stated your question implies that your own self-esteem is none too high. Why do I get the feeling that you see yourself as a lowly homemaker in a world of women lawyers and athletes and congresswomen? Do you feel inferior to women in the business world? Is it possible that you feel fortunate to have

"captured" your good-looking, successful man and wonder
how long the illusion will last? If these are secret weaknesses
in your self-concept, they will be reflected in your relationship with your husband. He will sense your fearfulness—
your unhealthy dependence—your "unworthiness" of his
love. You must believe that you bring as much to the family
as your husband does and that not only are you fortunate
to be married to Dwight, but he's a pretty lucky guy, too.

\* \* \*

All right, now it's final examination time. You have sat in
my course on *love must be tough* for an entire semester, and
the time has come to demonstrate what you've learned. Provided
below is a test—a prototype letter drawn from thousands I receive. Read it and answer the questions that follow as you think
I would, and then express your own views on the issues.

Dear Dr. Dobson:
I hope you can take a few minutes and try to help me. I feel
really desperate, and I'm praying that you have some answer for
me.
My husband and I were married very young, and after about
four years he started running around. That lasted for a couple of
years before he became a Christian. Then for six years things were
fine. He is an insurance salesman and did quite well financially.
But then he had an affair with a woman in our church. It only
lasted a short time—and the other members did not find out about
it. We moved to another town to get away from her. From then
on, it was one woman after another, ending with my next-door
neighbor. He moved in and out of the house on four occasions.
He settled back in last September and hasn't left since, although
the affair with my neighbor didn't end. We have been trying to
get our marriage back together since then, but I'm finding it's getting
harder instead of easier for me. My mind is in a turmoil.
I cannot accept it when he says to me, "I love you." (He does
not know any of these feelings and does not seem willing to discuss
anything either.) I'm torn. I don't know what to do. For years,
my great fear has been, "When will it happen again?" And very

soon, it does. Would I be better off with him or without him? The other woman is the total opposite of me spiritually. She and her three children have now moved in my house to stay, which I sometimes find unbearable. (This other woman's husband divorced her.)

Dr. Dobson, my mind is so full of questions and I guess one of the main problems is, "What are his true feelings for this woman?" Sometimes he just sits so quietly and of course I think his mind is on her. He's thirty-eight now and if I truly believed his problems were the "change of life," I could probably handle it better. But I see it more as a lifelong pattern.

Sex is super important to my husband, I think to a fault. He tells me he has "no complaints" where I'm concerned. One remark he made once was, "I always come back to you; that should tell you something."

He will not allow me to work (I may look at someone else), and he does not believe in counseling and would be furious if he knew I was writing to you.

I'm so torn I don't know what to do. Our whole family has been devastated by this and I feel like Satan has made a real bid for all of us.

What should I do to straighten out my marriage?

Mary

## Final Examination

1. List the mistakes Mary has made; underline the *first* and most serious one.
2. What is her husband probably thinking now?
3. How does he see his wife?
4. Mary's husband said, "I always come back to you; that should tell you something." What does it tell her?
5. Mary is not permitted to work for fear she will find another man. What does this say about the power she possesses with her husband?
6. Will her husband continue to cheat?

7. Why do you suppose Mary has permitted her husband to behave as he wished?
8. Can this marriage be saved?
9. What would you advise Mary to do?

## DOBSON'S ANSWERS

1. Mary made seven mistakes by my count:
   a. *She apparently failed to create a crisis when her husband's first act of infidelity occurred, permitting it to continue for two years.*
   b. She cooperated in the concealment of his second affair with a church member. If he had repented, it would have been best to keep the affair a secret. In the absence of that contrition, perhaps the pastor should have been approached.
   c. She permitted him to move in and out of the house like a yo-yo, allowing him to return without any commitment to be faithful. Indeed, his affair with a neighbor continued without interruption.
   d. She concealed her own feelings about his phony concept of love. Neither did she tell him about her great fears of his continued unfaithfulness. Why? Because she was appeasing her husband. He might have left if she dared to complain. This woman could easily be the "saint" we read about earlier in the song "She's Got To Be A Saint."
   e. Alas, she allowed the other woman and her three children to move into her house permanently!
   f. She continued to meet her husband's sexual needs as though nothing had happened. He was joyfully jumping from one bed to the other, apparently.
   g. She permitted this unfaithful, disrespectful man to continue as her leader ("He will not allow me to work"). She should have been preparing herself for economic survival if he decided to abandon her.

   By the foregoing measures, Mary demonstrated *weak* love. What she desperately needed was loving toughness!

2. He's trying to decide whether or not to leave his wife.

3. He sees her as a good woman, but as a pathetic pushover who will let him escape with murder. He disrespects her profoundly.

4. It tells her (1) that he still cares for her, in a manner of speaking, and (2) that he disrespects her. His statement puts him in the position of a master tossing a bone to a grateful dog. She should tell him, "Who needs it?"

5. This statement is *the* most important line in the letter. If I were counseling Mary, I would build an entire strategy on the implications of those words. What it says, in effect, is that this man cares enough about Mary to be jealous of her. He doesn't want anyone else to even know her! This should give her the confidence to call his bluff and lay the relationship on the line. I believe he would yield in a crisis.

6. Yes, unless Mary takes his toys away.

7. She is terrified—of loneliness, rejection, divorce, financial ruin, single parenthood, embarrassment, physical violence, and the unknown. She also suffers from massive low self-esteem which keeps her immobilized.

8. More than likely, it *can* be saved. Much depends on Mary's courage.

9. Mary should ask her loose lover to leave and take his girl-friend (and her three kids) with him. Let him play with his harem until he's sick of life on the road. She should get a job and prepare for a long winter. When (and if) he comes home with a desire to reconcile, I would advise them to completely reconstruct their relationship with the help of a Christian counselor. And of course, Mary should pray without ceasing.

# 10.
# *Victims of Affairs: A Dialogue*

**S**ince our purpose herein is to discover the fundamental causes of marital erosion and divorce, it seems appropriate that we continue to look closely at families that have experienced this tragedy. If a medical scientist wishes to understand the effects of typhus or emphysema or ulcers, he carefully examines patients who are afflicted with those diseases. Accordingly, we must focus our attention on marriages that have been invaded by the "bacteria" of interpersonal conflict—the most infectious disease of our time.

Toward that end, I invited four intelligent, highly verbal people into our radio studio to talk about their experiences with infidelity. The program, "Focus on the Family," is heard daily on 450 U.S. radio stations and more than 250 overseas. Each in his or her own way is a victim of an affair, having been betrayed by an unfaithful spouse. What follows in this chapter are portions of the transcript from that intense two-hour conversation involving three women and a man. Their stories are symbolic of millions in the Western world today and will serve to illustrate the principles I've tried to address.

May I suggest as you read these personal accounts that you attempt to correlate the details with our discussion to this point? Our purpose is not to embarrass the anonymous participants, of course, who have graciously given me permission to present their cases. Rather, we want to learn from them. Therefore, I hope you will look for common mistakes and errors in judgment, especially in the early stages of infidelity. Watch for panic and appeasement as the participants weave their way through their stories. Ask yourself if longsuffering and tolerance were successful in healing relationships. And finally, postulate your recommendations for those who are currently enduring a trial by fire. I will provide a commentary on the discussions in the following chapter.*

DOBSON:   I'd like to begin by paying special tribute to the four of you who've joined us in the studio today. It won't be easy to talk about the break-up of your families, but we can profit from what you learned as victims of infidelity. It goes without saying that this topic is a heavy one. Only this morning I heard about a woman whose husband left her. She cried almost incessantly for twelve months, and last Thursday, her thirteen-year-old daughter tried to commit suicide. That is where infidelity sometimes leads. But then, who would know that better than the four of you?

Let me begin by introducing you to our radio listeners. You've asked that I not use your real names, so we'll call you Sue, Jean, Mary Ann, and Mike. And I'm going to ask you, Mary Ann, to begin by telling us your story.

MARY ANN:   All right. Shortly after George and I were married, we lived at the beach and I taught school. My husband was unemployed and had too much free time on his hands. He obviously had a lot of female friends I didn't know, because in the evening he would get phone calls from these other women. I would ask him about the callers but he would never respond. Of course, I was feeling so much pain because we were married but not living in a marital relationship. We were living as roommates, due to, I'm sure, the guilt he had over his affairs.

---

* The comments have been edited for clarity and grammatical accuracy.

DOBSON: How long had you been married?

MARY ANN: We had been married for about six months when this began. Our divorce occurred after three and one-half years. It was very painful.

DOBSON: Do I understand that you tolerated what you knew to be blatant infidelity for that period of time?

MARY ANN: I knew it in my heart but—

DOBSON: You didn't really want to know it.

MARY ANN: Yes, right, exactly. I made a decision to say, "No, it's not really happening."

DOBSON: Was your husband unemployed by choice?

MARY ANN: It was by choice. The beach was too alluring. And the beautiful girls out there were, I'm sure, even more alluring to him.

DOBSON: Just how obvious was the infidelity? Did he ever bring women home with him?

MARY ANN: No, he didn't. He was very discreet. It was just that he didn't want to touch me or have anything to do with me. That was very painful. When your husband shows no interest, you feel like you have no worth and that you're very unattractive.

DOBSON: Did you and your husband share the same values before you were married? Did you think he was a Christian?

MARY ANN: My former husband and I dated *eight* years before we married!

DOBSON: Eight years!

MARY ANN: Yes. My parents had been divorced and I wanted to make sure that I was not getting into a bad marriage.

DOBSON: And you still got a surprise?

MARY ANN: I was—

DOBSON: Blind?

MARY ANN: Very blind, I guess. You know, I really believed that he loved the Lord. Now I know that he was living a double life during all those years we dated. But I had no knowledge of it. He was the first person who really loved me, I thought. I didn't get love from my home. I was twenty-four years old and I was educated and had my profession, so I really felt like I knew what I was doing. I really thought I knew this person. But, a month after we were married, it all came apart. The difficult thing, of course, is to try to go back and relive that decision. We had met at a Christian college and I believed in him. He believed in himself. There certainly wasn't any suggestion of danger then, nor did anyone else perceive it. Then when the affairs began, I would go back in my dreams at night, what little I could sleep, and re-examine my decision to marry. I was committed to God; I wasn't out of fellowship with Him. Despite my caution, I made an enormous mistake.

DOBSON:    Sue, I understand you thought you married a Christian too?

SUE:    Oh, I would have staked my life on it. And in fact, I did. We had been married, let's see, probably fifteen years before I ever knew he was playing around. At that time he was an administrator in a Christian college where I was teaching. He was also chairman of a moral action committee in our church, which is very ironic. When I learned he was involved in an affair, I could say nothing to anyone because our pastor, our college president, his colleagues . . . were all my friends too. I just couldn't ruin his reputation with them. It was a terrible time.

DOBSON:    How long were the affairs going on before you knew?

SUE:    I'm not sure. I was very spaced out until I finally faced reality. After that, the affairs were continuous until finally the marriage was dissolved. That was a period of six years.

DOBSON:    Like Mary Ann, you knowingly tolerated your husband's infidelity for six years?

SUE:    Yes. As a Christian I just committed myself more strongly to the marriage; I was determined that if there were any way to make it work, with God's help, I was going to do that.

DOBSON:    But you lost it anyway?

SUE: Yes.

DOBSON: Looking back on the experience, would there have been any way to have saved your home?

SUE: I don't think so. And, of course, by being patient I was able to give my children their father for six more years. They loved him best of anyone in the world and still have a good image of him. I wouldn't change that.

DOBSON: Mike, tell me your story.

MIKE: Well, I had a very successful marriage until my wife had a severe accident and a concussion which left her totally incapable of functioning from January to the end of that school year. She was a teacher, and during that lengthy period of time where she could not function, I took over most of the responsibilities of the home. The next year the doctors felt that for her own self-image, she needed to return to teaching, which she really wanted to do. But she was not emotionally or physically ready. She needed somebody to lean on. That somebody happened to teach next door. Their friendship just evolved from there.

DOBSON: Could you see it coming?

MIKE: At first I couldn't, but during the next two years, I sensed that she was drawing away from me. When we would try to talk about it, we just went around in circles and never seemed to come to a conclusion. I couldn't figure out what I was dealing with. I had trusted her implicitly for seventeen years. We had had a happy marriage and to even imagine that she was unfaithful was unthinkable.

SUE: It's almost impossible to believe you've been betrayed when you've committed your life to another person.

DOBSON: Especially in the Christian context.

MARY ANN: Absolutely.

DOBSON: You all were involved in church-going families—

SUE: Yes. In fact, the worst part of the experience for me was the loss of my spiritual leader. I could handle the rejection and the treachery better than I could deal with the implications of James's sin.

DOBSON: Jean, let's hear your story.

JEAN: I identify with what Sue just said. That loss of the person that I looked up to spiritually was the hardest part for me, too. My husband was a career churchman, so I not only lost my mate and the father of my children, but I felt like I lost my spiritual leader.

DOBSON: That's interesting. Both you and Sue experienced the same thing.

JEAN: Oh, it was my whole lifestyle. Divorce is different than just losing a person; you lose your way of life.

DOBSON: How did it happen to you, Jean?

JEAN: Well, I feel like the senior member here. We lost our marriage after thirty-two years, which is really a tragedy. In fact, that's why I'm here today. If you go through a tragedy you ought to be able to use it to help someone else, and I hope my story will do that. The reason I was so attracted to Maury (and in fact, I still am) was that he was the most moral, sincere kind of boy that I had ever dated. We married when we were both nineteen, and we had children right away. He had his first affair, a short little one, when we had two children. I was very upset about it, naturally. I confronted him, and we decided to treat this like modern people would do. So the four of us, two husbands and two wives, sat down and talked about it. Maury was terribly sorry about the whole thing. He really was. It was not the kind of thing that a man with his background would want to do. And so, all was forgiven and the matter ended. He also had another little encounter, just a little kind of an evening thing, at a party one night, but that blew over too. Right after that, Maury began his career and we went along as a very normal, happy family. Then about ten or fifteen years ago, I guess, I found out that he was involved in an affair with someone else. I was ill at the time, and Maury is a very sensitive man. He said he was lonely and needed another woman to do what I couldn't do for him at the time.

DOBSON: Did you buy that?

JEAN:  At the time I did. Yes and no. I wanted to believe him because he really was such a good man. But his extramarital activity continued. He had a long-term affair where he saw a woman regularly for nearly two years. It was not a sexual affair. But it was just as painful to me.

DOBSON:  An emotional affair?

JEAN:  That's right. I felt a greater sense of disloyalty over that, picturing him sharing himself, than I would have if he had been sleeping with her. He had other affairs as the years went by—some occasionally with women of the street. I'm not sure you would call that kind of thing an affair.

DOBSON:  You knew about each involvement?

JEAN:  Yes. Sometimes a long period of time would go by before I found out. But I always found out.

DOBSON:  Mary Ann, didn't you tell me earlier that God revealed your husband's infidelity to you?

MARY ANN:  Yes, he did. I had attended a Christian seminar, and on the way home, I experienced a horrible grip of fear. I just knew I was going to go home and find my husband in bed with another girl. Then I said to myself, "Mary Ann! What in the world is wrong with you? That's ridiculous!"

DOBSON:  You had never caught him before?

MARY ANN:  No. That's why I condemned myself. Nevertheless, I confronted my husband when I got home. He became very angry and made me feel like I was really off the wall. But he *was* involved at the time and it was God's way of preparing me for what was to come. The Lord is so gentle in the way He deals with His children.

DOBSON:  Looking back on the first revelation, the moment when each of you first became aware that you had serious problems on your hands, how wisely do you feel you handled the situation? Was there anything you could have done that would have helped? Is there anything you'd do differently if you had those years to live over?

MARY ANN:  What I did wrong was that I didn't pray about the very thing I wanted so desperately. I reacted with anger.

Instead of saying, "Lord, show me what kind of wife George needs," I was always so spiritually dogmatic that my husband *had* to be the way he was. You know it takes two to make a marriage work and some of my actions didn't help accomplish that. My husband probably ran from the very thing I wanted him to do because I was so strong.

DOBSON: How is that?

MARY ANN: I was a very self-righteous Christian at that point, who loved the Lord with all her heart, soul, strength and mind.

DOBSON: How can you blame yourself for that, Mary Ann?

MARY ANN: Well, nothing is wrong with that, but I handled it wrong. I would say to him, "Please read the Bible to me." You know, sometimes I'd be into the Word of God, and really wanting to seek after Truth, and he'd try to distract me. I remember making a comment I'll never forget. It's the worst thing a woman can do. I said, "You're a tool of Satan!" It was horrible. So there were many things I did wrong that God has revealed to me over the years. I thank the Lord that He only revealed them to me very gradually.

SUE: The main mistake I made was becoming very cold, sexually. My husband was so cruel and rough, and I had gotten to where I just couldn't respond. But the moment his infidelity was revealed, I was able to be warm and loving again. I asked his forgiveness immediately. That was my first response when I got the news. I think that's why I became suicidal. I felt so guilty; I knew I had caused the affairs. But then when I did everything I could to make up for those mistakes and the infidelity continued, then I didn't feel as guilty. But that first year after learning about his unfaithfulness was awful. I cried every day for twelve months. I'm sure I was a wonderful blessing to my husband during that time. By then we had five little children and it was so hard to manage the home and be a professional person as he wanted me to be. I wish I could have stopped crying but I didn't know what else to do. And there was no one in our environment to whom I could turn. The church counselors were his friends. There was no one. I couldn't talk to his parents or mine. It was terrible.

DOBSON: Sue, that says so much about your character . . . about who you are. Your primary concern was for his reputation, even when your own pain took you to the threshold of suicide. You had every right to seek counsel from someone!

SUE: Yes, but I was afraid that whoever I talked to would come back to the school and then his reputation would be ruined.

DOBSON: Well, that shows the extent of your courage. But I would not have advised it.

SUE: I did call his mother a few times that spring, but my husband said, "Don't you ever talk to Mom about this again." So I honored his orders. I said I would not.

DOBSON: Jean, what mistakes did you make during the time of crisis?

JEAN: I was angry and my ego was hurt and I handled it terribly. There were many confrontations and demands that the affairs stop. But it was all wrong. After Maury and I became Christians (we were baptized holding hands), our marriage stabilized and there was a long period of time, maybe fifteen years or so, before there was any other instance of infidelity. I always thought it would never happen again, you know, because he was so sorry. We would talk about his unfaithfulness and he would be so sorry. Usually, he would only get in trouble during times when his career was at a really low point. I felt I understood why he did it. I didn't like it, but I understood him; I concluded that he was a man who wasn't very verbal, and he couldn't talk about the pain he felt about his career and where he fit into the world.

SUE: My ex-husband had that problem too.

JEAN: So I felt that he went and looked for another woman to kind of give him a little boost.

SUE: That's exactly my experience too. My husband could be open with me when he was emotionally up, but in those low times he needed to go find someone else to get high with, I think, because he was so nonverbal and it was very hard for him to open up.

DOBSON: Mike, looking back on your trials, what mistakes did you make?

MIKE: Well, finally when I found out about the affair, it did not come as a surprise. I confronted my wife and she denied it. Then I got in touch with the wife of the man that she was involved with, and it was confirmed.

DOBSON: How did you react?

MIKE: I waited six days before confronting her. Then I said that I knew what she had told me the previous week had not been true.

DOBSON: Why did you wait so long to confront her?

MIKE: A friend advised me not to react the night I got the news. He told me to think it over and seek God's guidance about how I should deal with the problem. It's probably the best advice I got. I'm convinced that that is the best thing I could have done because I got myself ready to accept and face whatever I needed to deal with, realizing I loved her. But my mistake was in not recognizing sooner what was going on. When I would say, "I love you," and I did not get a loving response back, that should have been my clue. I should have asked her if she loved me.

DOBSON: If she wouldn't admit her involvement when she was knee deep in an affair, would she have confessed no matter what you said or did?

MIKE: At one point she might have. I remember I told her I loved her and she looked at me and said, "Mike, you have a very confused wife." I dropped the subject. I felt like she didn't want to talk about it, but I should have pursued it with her.

JEAN: It is hard to know what would be helpful.

MIKE: That's it. You question everything.

*Note the next comment. It is significant to our discussion.*

SUE: Another mistake I made was in not knowing how to confront. I now think I understand what might have been a better approach. My sister went through a similar experience. Neither she nor her husband was a Christian. She had been very soft-spoken and passive, but she became stronger overnight. She asked her husband to move out and get an apartment, which he did. Within a year he decided his family was most important and he came home. I looked at that and wished I could have found a Biblical basis to do something similar.

DOBSON: Sue, I have seen that happen more times than I can count, where loving toughness and confrontation brought responsibility in marriage—in the same way that they do between a parent and a child or in any other relationship in life. There is a place in marriage for one partner to say to the other, "Rick, I love you. We married one another of our own free will; no one forced us to become husband and wife. We dedicated ourselves to one another exclusively and it must continue to be that way. If you can't be faithful to me for life, then I'd rather separate right now. I cannot be one of many lovers. It must be all or nothing. If you choose to leave me I will be severely hurt, because my love for you is very deep. Let me say it one more time so you will understand exactly how I feel. I want you as my husband more than anything in the world, and if you can pledge yourself to me for the rest of our lives together, I'll do my best to forgive and forget. But if not, then there's no better time than right now for you to leave with one of your girlfriends." Do you understand the wisdom of a firm stance like that? Does it make sense to you?

JEAN: Oh, yes, I understand it now. At one point toward the latter years of our marriage, Maury got involved with yet another woman that he didn't tell me about. She called our home and I found out they were meeting. I was a stronger person at that time than I was when I was younger, and I said to Maury, "All right, I will give you a divorce and you can pursue the relationship." He said, "No, I don't want you to divorce me; I just want some freedom to see where this relationship is going." I said, "No, that won't work. If you go with this woman, I will divorce you." He said, "I don't want that," and he cut off the relationship.

DOBSON: That is precisely my point. If when you were younger, you had been able to apply that kind of toughness after the first act of unfaithfulness, instead of years later when the damage had been done, you might have saved your marriage.

MIKE: Later on I realized that I should have been tougher. But I struggled with guilt for a long time. My father-in-law is a minister and I love him very dearly, but he contributed to my self-condemnation. He wanted so badly to see the marriage continue because of his own pain. He wrote to me listing all the Scriptures that said divorce was wrong. I agreed, but I had no choice in the matter! I eventually saw that it wasn't my fault.

SUE: Oh, I felt so guilty, too. I felt that maybe it was all my fault and if I had been a better wife he wouldn't have looked somewhere else. If I had been more understanding, if I had been more perceptive—all of these things. So I forgave him time after time. I have to say I still feel married; I feel like a married single. I don't know whether time will dispel that or not.

DOBSON: Did all of you deal with bitterness?

MARY ANN: Oh, definitely.

SUE: I was bitter initially, but I forgave immediately. Then James got involved again. So I thought, okay, if I am like Christ and absolutely sacrificial in my love, perhaps that will be attractive to him. But it wasn't. I mean I can say I was absolutely sacrificial for six years!

DOBSON: Let me ask an important question. It has been my observation in dealing with people who have been through what you have experienced that the unfaithful partner typically tries to expunge his guilt by refocusing the blame. He tells

his spouse that their marriage should never have occurred
. . . that he didn't love her even in the beginning . . . that
the divorce is really an act of kindness . . . that it wouldn't
have happened if his spouse hadn't caused the problems . . .
that their breakup is actually in the best interest of the kids
. . . and that God Himself has approved of the divorce. Did
your partners give you these phony messages?

SUE:   Oh, all of them, especially the one about God's approval.
My ex-husband's present wife, the one with whom he had
an affair, is also a Christian college teacher. I felt the Lord
wanted me to go to her and ask her forgiveness for my bad
attitude. She had been my friend for twenty years, and it
was extremely difficult to approach her, but I did and I told
her I had forgiven her for what had happened. She then
told me that she and my ex-husband had prayed about their
marriage and received assurance from God that it was right.

DOBSON:   That is the ultimate rationalization. It makes blatant
sin sound sanctified, but only for a time. A day of accountability is coming.

SUE:   Yes, I suggested to my friend that she look a little closer
at what the Scripture says about keeping the marriage bed
undefiled, and other passages. She said, "Oh, no, I don't
believe in reading the Bible too closely because it is subject
to so many *interpretations.*"

JEAN:   The real crusher is when your unfaithful husband says,
"But I really love you, I really do. This affair is something
that has happened outside of our relationship. It is irrelevant.
We still love one another and shouldn't let this problem affect
us." You feel at times like you are almost going insane because
these contradictory messages are given back to back.

SUE:   That is what caused me to have a serious breakdown.

DOBSON:   You said you were suicidal, Sue. Were you, Mary
Ann?

MARY ANN:   Yes, I was.

DOBSON:   Did anybody else think of suicide?

MIKE:   Yes.

SUE:   I had been a Christian since I was a preschooler but I still was suicidal when all of this happened. My husband said, "You think God is so great; why isn't He helping you?" I had sense enough to say that I knew He would if I could let Him, but I was hurting so badly I couldn't stop shouting. I later read a book by C. S. Lewis called *A Grief Observed,* and he experienced the same inability to accept God's grace when he went through the death of his wife. That really ministered to me. A number of books have helped me.

JEAN:   Can I tell you something wonderful that happened to me? During my period of suicidal tendencies, my older daughter died from a terminal illness. She left a supply of her medication and I looked at those pills and knew there were enough to take my life. I was at the end of my rope, and I was counting the pills when the phone rang. It was a friend who offered to come over. I didn't want to see him and said I wouldn't let him in. He asked what he could do for me, and I said, "Nothing, there is no reason to go any further." He talked to me and prayed with me, but you know, I was so distressed that I couldn't hear him. I couldn't even hear the Scripture he read. After I hung up the phone, he began calling different people, some who knew me and some who didn't. Those people called me all night long. They either prayed with me or just talked with me every hour. That's how I got through the night. . . .

MIKE:   That is wonderful!

JEAN:   It was at the same time the worst and best night of my life.

DOBSON:   In listening to the four of you share your individual pain, I am impressed again by the willingness of loving people to blame themselves for things they couldn't help. Each of you did the best you could to cope with irresponsibility and unfaithfulness in your spouses. Even though you made mistakes and were imperfect marriage partners, you were the ones who did everything you could to hold things together. Nevertheless, you blamed yourselves, felt incredible guilt, suffered low self-esteem, and even wanted to die for your failures. Doesn't that seem a bit unfair to yourselves?

SUE: Yes, but that's the way I felt. I had to work through it.

JEAN: Yes!

MIKE: I definitely felt like that. Another thing that makes you feel so terrible is that you are alone but your unfaithful spouse is in the arms of another lover. You walk into the church you have attended for years with her and you sit in the pew where the two of you used to worship. The building begins to close in on you, even though you are surrounded by people. You feel a kind of panic sweeping over you.

DOBSON: Mike, did you deal with bitterness?

MIKE: Oh, yes! I didn't realize just how bitter I was. That's why I couldn't talk to my boys about what was going on. They had never heard their mom or me fight, and they didn't know until the night before she left that she was leaving. Now I know why I couldn't sit down and explain everything to them. I would have conveyed my bitterness to them. Then after my wife had been gone for about four months, I knew it was time to tell the boys the whole story. I was afraid someone at church would tell them if I didn't. It needed to come from me.

DOBSON: How did they take it?

MIKE: Well, it was more difficult for the younger one. He had always turned to his mother. In fact, he had really been her favorite.

DOBSON: Did it make him bitter?

MIKE: Very bitter. It was extremely difficult to deal with. He did not know how to handle it. He went through one very, very bad year in school. But he has come to me since then and said, "I am sorry that the divorce took place, but at least it helped me get to know you." And I am glad for that.

DOBSON: Did he cry himself to sleep in the early days?

MIKE: Yes.

DOBSON: Did he bite his nails? Did he wake up in the middle

of the night? Did he have an upset stomach? Did he have headaches? What were the other symptoms?

MIKE: There were headaches; there were days when he didn't feel like going to school; there were attendance problems. There were other stresses we *all* had to deal with. Finally, we talked one night and I said, "Guys, I think right now we need to recognize that we are all going through some terrible times, and so when we are down, let's just be honest and say, 'Hey, today I am in the pits. Don't bug me; just leave me alone. I really need your support today.'" The three of us learned to do this. It was amazing how, when we began to pull together, God helped us love one another and survive the crisis.

SUE: It has been eight years for my children, and my boy was a special problem. He ran away from home and got into the gay scene. It was terrible for a time. But now he's married and has two little kids. But all our children went through some depression. One of our girls had epileptic seizures until we found out it was caused by depression, and then she was able to control it. All of them are still suffering from some of these things.

DOBSON: Mary Ann, you didn't have children when all this took place, did you?

MARY ANN: No. I was married at twenty-four, but I chose not to be a mother. I never wanted to have children. I love kids, but some of my background from my own family had frightened me. Now I have two little girls with my second husband and I love them to pieces.

DOBSON: Jean, how did your five children make it?

JEAN: My oldest daughter died just before we separated.

DOBSON: So you went through the divorce and the death at almost the same time. How did you handle that?

JEAN: I think I handled the death fine. That may sound strange, but it is a wonderful memory. My daughter had cancer of the brain, but she went into remission during the summer months—as though God gave us an unexpected gift. My husband and I were very close during that time. We supported each other well against death; we just couldn't face life. . . .

DOBSON:   What happened after your daughter's death?

JEAN:   He filed for divorce. Once she was gone, there was very little to hold us together.

DOBSON:   What was the effect of the divorce on the rest of your kids?

JEAN:   There have been lasting effects. I have a son, a fine young man who was engaged to be married to a lovely girl this past year. But three days before the wedding, they canceled their plans. They were both scared. They both came from divorced families. They love each other and are still very close; in fact, they are still engaged to be married. But they are afraid to take that step. And, of course, my other teenage son just could not handle the divorce at all. He is still having counseling and—

DOBSON:   Is he bitter at his father?

JEAN:   No, he is not bitter. All of my children were very protective of their father. Their father was a very fragile man, and they didn't know about any of the uglier part of our marriage. They just knew that we didn't get along and that we led rather separate lives toward the end. I think I made a big mistake, I have to say, in a moment of bitterness and certainly in poor judgment. I told the whole story about the affair to my oldest daughter who is twenty-eight. It only made her angry at me.

DOBSON:   At you?

JEAN:   At me. She did not want to hear that. She didn't want her boat rocked, you know, and it has taken us a long time to mend.

SUE:   My son blamed me at first but he sees now that it wasn't my fault. The girls were very shocked, but they supported me.

MARY ANN:   I was the child of a broken marriage where infidelity had occurred. My mother tried to get my support by putting my father down and telling me some truths that were too painful for me to receive. I immediately went to my father's side.

JEAN:   It is awful to place immature children in that vise!

SUE:   That's why I always sought ways to honor the father and tried to figure out ways to do that. I admit it was difficult at times.

MIKE:   My younger son finally said, "You know, if mom is going to get back into the proper relationship with God, it may only come through my brother or me."

SUE:   Yes, my girls have said the same thing.

DOBSON:   Each of you has talked about feeling bitterness, guilt, low self-esteem, and other negative emotions. It is surprising, though, that very little has been said about anger. Mary Ann, did you harbor a great deal of hostility over your husband's unfaithfulness?

MARY ANN:   Well, as a Christian I didn't feel that anger was right, so I wanted to suppress it as long as I possibly could until my husband finally asked me to leave. And I said, "God, could this really be your will, having him ask me to leave again?" I mean, I'm a glutton for punishment, obviously, but I wanted to know for sure.

DOBSON:   Now let's get it straight. Your husband was having multiple affairs with his beach friends. He was unemployed, not even looking for a job. You were paying the bills and bailing him out of jail and getting calls from his girlfriends. Yet he asked *you* to get out!

MARY ANN:   That's right. When he asked me to leave the first time I remember just running out of the house in tears. I had no place to go. I didn't care if I lived or died. I was extremely angry at God. I'll never forget shaking my fist at Him and saying, "God! You said in Your Word that You would work all things together for those who love You and are called according to Your purpose, and I love You! But this is *not* good in my life and I can't stand it!"

DOBSON:   And so your anger was directed not at your husband but at God?

MARY ANN:   That's right. I realize now when I look back that most of us have to deal with anger in some way. I did it in my closet, so to speak.

DOBSON:   You didn't tell anybody?

MARY ANN:   No one. Not even my parents.

DOBSON:   How do you think God received your anger at that time?

MARY ANN:   Very lovingly. He wrapped His arms around me and let me cry and express my anger like a child.

DOBSON:   I'm sure He did, Mary Ann. He saw you as a frightened little girl who'd been terribly hurt. You thought you had found a man to love you and go through life with, but suddenly you were thrown out into the night with no place to go and no one even to talk to. The loving God we serve must have felt immeasurable compassion and tenderness toward you at that moment.

MARY ANN:   I know He did. The verse that He gave me was in Psalms 30:5. "Weeping comes in the evening but joy comes in the morning." I would have never known the extent of God's love if I had not gone through this trial.

DOBSON:   As a matter of fact, you told me God wrote you a love letter at that time.

MARY ANN:   Yes, he directed me to a second passage in Isaiah 54 that became His love letter to me. I was angry at God, not only because of the pain He permitted me to experience, but because I was embarrassed in front of my students. They knew I was a Christian and yet I had to admit to them that I had gotten a divorce. I wanted to run—to escape to Australia or somewhere. Then the Lord assured me that it was His reputation at stake and He would take care of it. He then gave me this beautiful passage of Scripture.

> "Do not be afraid; you will not suffer shame.
>     Do not fear disgrace; you will not be humiliated.
> You will forget the shame of your youth
>     and remember no more the reproach of your widowhood.
> For your Maker is your husband—
>     the Lord Almighty is his name—
> the Holy One of Israel is your Redeemer;
>     he is called the God of all the earth.

The Lord will call you back
  as if you were a wife deserted and distressed in spirit—
a wife who married young,
  only to be rejected," says your God.
"For a brief moment I abandoned you,
  but with deep compassion I will bring you back.
In a surge of anger
  I hid my face from you for a moment,
but with everlasting kindness
  I will have compassion on you,"
  says the Lord your Redeemer.

Isaiah 54:4–8, NIV

That Scripture was so relevant to my need that it could easily have begun with the words, "Dear Mary Ann." I was that young and rejected wife who felt forsaken by God. But He gathered me and embraced me in His everlasting love.

DOBSON:   That is beautiful, Mary Ann. Do you still believe all things work together for good to them that love God?

MARY ANN:   Oh, yes!

DOBSON:   Even for those whose spouses get into affairs?

MARY ANN:   You know, I can say this honestly. If I had to do it over again I'd do it the same way, because I love who I am today. When I was rejected and left alone I was able to love myself for the very first time because I knew I was loved by God.

SUE:   I had a pastor say to me, "How can you stand all of this?" And I said, "Because I really like myself. I know what I am in God's sight." And that was the thing that sustained me!

JEAN:   No one wants to suffer and have her foundations crumble, but God made me strong through these things. He held me and let me grow in strength, and you know, I've lost a child—had a lot of tragedy in our family. I've had a breakdown, I've had a divorce, I've had a suicidal child, but God has been there as my rock.

SUE:   That's exactly the way I feel. It's been eight years and

I still have to lean on the Lord. All I can say is, "I am content in my circumstances this day." I had a friend who said, "But I don't have the gift of celibacy." I just laughed. To someone who's been married twenty years, that was hilarious. Who *does* have the gift of celibacy? But God is giving me the grace to cope with single parenting and all the other stresses. You know, I wasn't cut out for this role. I'm not a good president; I'm a good vice president, a helper. But my family is doing fine and I'm in one piece. I don't understand the tragedy in my life, but I'm stronger than I would have been without it.

MIKE:    I went through a divorce the same year I was demoted in my work. I had been a counselor in a junior high school for fifteen years. Then my job was eliminated at the end of that term and I was sent back to the classroom. That was embarrassing. Suddenly, every prop that we call "success" was literally knocked out from under me and my trust for the first time *had* to be totally on the Lord. I had trusted Him before, but now I was powerless to do anything else. Like the rest of you, I became a very strong person during this time of challenge. I continue to be amazed at how much God loves us and seeks us out wherever we are.

JEAN:    You know, my children are proud of me, too. All of my married life I was a homemaker. I never felt I had a choice to have a career. I was a wife and a mother and that was my role in life. When the divorce occurred, I had never worked a day outside the home. I didn't have any skills or any great talent. I didn't have a college education! But I took hold and God kept saying, "You can do it! You can do it!" It looked impossible. I didn't know how to get a job or how to support myself. I didn't even know how to balance the checkbook. But God was there and I'm proud of what I've accomplished. He let me be a bigger person than I used to be.

DOBSON:    I'm sure the four of you realize you are talking to many people by means of radio today who are going through the agony you experienced in the past. Someone is listening who has recently discovered that a beloved husband or wife is involved in an affair. That person feels like life is over, but what you're saying is, "You can make it, and even though it feels like God is unconcerned, He really does care!"

JEAN:  That's why I accepted your invitation to be here today. I wanted to help someone who is suffering the way I did.

DOBSON:  You have all done that during these broadcasts, and I've learned to love each of you through our conversations. On behalf of our listeners, I thank you for opening these old wounds and letting us feel your pain. Your faith and courage have been an inspiration to us all.

# 11.
# *Discussion of the Dialogue*

*I*'m sure the reader was impressed, as was I, by the ability of Mary Ann, Sue, Jean and Mike to articulate their experiences and feelings. I respect each of them highly and have profited from their insights and observations. Nevertheless, it is surprising to me that these four intelligent people still have very little comprehension of the forces that destroyed their marriages (although I have seen the same "blindness" in many others who have faced similar circumstances.)

A key ingredient in the erosion of their homes was a kind of marital permissiveness which proved to be fatal. Upon learning that their spouses were involved in affairs, their instinctive reaction was to understand, to explain, to forgive or to ignore the adultery occurring under their noses. These good people were motivated by committed love in its purest form and I admire them for their compassion under the most awful pressure. Nevertheless, they each found "excuses" for the unfaithfulness of their partners, which permitted the disloyal behavior to continue unchecked.

Mary Ann felt she was too righteous, saying, "I was so spiritually dogmatic that my husband *had* to be the way he was." Sue blamed James's infidelity on her own sexual unresponsiveness. (May I ask, who wouldn't be cooled off by his "cruel and rough" treatment?) Jean attributed one of Maury's affairs to her illness. Mike thought his wife's car wreck was the key factor. Then they agreed that business reverses, low self-esteem and communicative problems were instrumental. Perhaps they are right—perhaps there *were* mitigating circumstances in each case. But no one labeled the behavior for what it was: selfishness and sin!

Therein lies a fundamental problem. These loving, gracious people inadvertently shielded their wayward spouses from the consequences of infidelity. If there is *anything* that an adulterer does not need, it is a guilt-ridden mate who understands his indiscretion and assumes the blame for it. Such a person needs to be called to *accountability,* not excused by rationalization! That's why being married to a tolerant, compassionate husband or wife who instantly forgives and forgets can give an infidel a one-way ticket to hell! And I mean that literally.

I want to be careful not to imply condemnation and criticism of the four members of our discussion group. They are admirable people who are made out of better stuff than I am. I sat in awe as I observed the tenacity with which they faced their problems. I ached for each of them as they groped to explain what had gone wrong, and how the blame somehow always managed to bounce back in their faces. But I disagreed with many of their conclusions, and in fact, believe their early tolerance played a role in the divorces that subsequently occurred.

Not only did these four victims (they dislike that name but I don't know how else to label them) fail to confront their spouses with loving toughness, but they also shielded them from emotional pain. That is unfortunate. Just as a rebellious pre-schooler can profit from a well-timed spanking, the psychological consequences of sinful behavior should be experienced by the guilty. There's nothing quite like a dose of reality to awaken a dreamer from his fantasies. Nevertheless, the four infidels were protected from those important consequences.

Remember that each of the victims diligently concealed the truth to preserve his or her partner's reputation. Though each case must be considered individually, especially where children are concerned, the degree of secrecy maintained in those instances seems unwarranted to me. It was almost masochistic of Sue and Mary Ann to tell *no one,* not a living soul, about the agony they were suffering in silence. Mike and Jean guarded their secrets as well. All four of them were taken to the brink of suicide.

Because of this concealment, other natural consequences of infidelity were avoided. The adulterer was under no gentle pressure from fellow Christians who would have reinforced responsible behavior; none of the offenders had to justify their conduct to their older children; none was asked to move into new and inconvenient living quarters; none, apparently, was denied sexual privileges from the rejected spouse (Sue even became warmer at the time of disclosure and immediately asked for forgiveness); none had to pay a marriage counselor; none had to support a lawyer (or two of them); none faced the financial pressures of maintaining two residences; and alas, none had to look himself in the mirror each morning and ask, "Why does everyone seem to think it's *my* fault?"

Under the circumstances, we should not be surprised that the affairs involving the three husbands continued through the years. (Mike's wife was in a different situation, but she still needed discovery and confrontation.) It should have been expected. The lure of infidelity is an *addiction* to an individual who has a chink in his moral armor. While some people are chemically dependent on alcohol or heroin or cocaine, this kind of infidel is hooked on illicit sex. Psychologically, he needs the thrill of the chase, the clandestine meetings, the forbidden fruit, the flattery, the sexual conquest, the proof of manhood or womanhood, and in some cases, the discovery. And like the drug abuser, he is constantly attempting to reform. He promises with sincerity never again to yield to his habit. But unless his entire social milieu acts to support that commitment, he is likely to forget it. In the case of the husbands of our three female guests, they were cradled in a forgiving and protective environment that encouraged and supported their folly. What they needed were wives who were committed to the concept that *love must be tough.*

There are other lessons to be learned from the experiences of the dialogue participants. Let's return to a question-and-answer format which will permit us to tease out those kernels of understanding.

Q. How can you say that the four victims of affairs failed to confront their unfaithful partners, when it is obvious from the dialogue that they had some incredible battles? Mary Ann described those conflicts as "horrible." Jean said she handled them "terribly," making many demands that Maury stop his infidelity. Isn't that what you mean by *confronting* the problem?

A. Unfortunately, it is not. Simply becoming angry and throwing temper tantrums is no more effective with a spouse than it is with a rebellious teenager. Screaming and accusing and berating are rarely successful in changing the behavior of human beings of *any* age. What is required is a course of *action*—an ultimatum that demands a specific response and results in a consequence. That is what didn't occur in the four homes we've heard described. None of the victims recognized the difference between expressions of anger and loving toughness. It is a common misunderstanding.

Q. I'm interested in Sue's comment that by tolerating her husband's infidelity, she permitted her children to have their father for six more years. At face value, that would imply that a victim of an affair should hold it all inside for the sake of the kids. This is different from your advice, of course. But what would you say to Sue? She *did* give her children their father for six more valuable years.

A. Again, I want to be gentle to Sue whom I admire greatly. Nevertheless, I feel her perspective was shortsighted. In the process of giving her children their father for a while longer, she also gave them a severely depressed, suicidal mother, and eventually, a family breakup. Her children continue to suffer today, as she indicated. Perhaps—perhaps if she had been tougher when the first affair occurred, she might have given the children their father for a lifetime. We'll never know, of course, but it could have happened.

Q. Sue also said she would have separated from her unfaithful husband if she could have found a Biblical basis to do so. Since you have recommended separation in response to some instances of infidelity, I wonder what scriptural support you have for that position.

A. At the end of this chapter I have provided a theological understanding of divorce and remarriage, as quoted from the writings of Dr. Chuck Swindoll. He refers to a passage in Matthew wherein Jesus made an exception to the permanence of the marital bond in instances of infidelity: "And I say to you, whoever divorces his wife, except for immorality, and marries another woman commits adultery" (19:9, RSV). I will leave it to Dr. Swindoll to explain that understanding. For our purposes here, let's accept it as stated, that is, divorce is permissible (but not mandatory) in instances of continued, unrepented, flagrant infidelity. If that is true, then a *separation* that is intended not to kill the marriage but to rescue it must also be lawful. If a person has Biblical grounds for divorce, he certainly would not be judged guilty for attempting to salvage the relationship through a painful process of separation. In this context, I believe that living apart for a period of time can clear the air for some families and permit the healing process to begin, especially where one partner is desperately in need of accountability. On the other hand, separation can destroy a marriage if done for the wrong reasons and in the wrong spirit.

Q. What about separation for reasons other than infidelity?

A. Again, I find no Biblical prohibition against couples living apart for a time, if their purpose is not to seek divorce and remarriage. As implied above, husbands and wives often trample on one another's nerves and desperately need some time alone to reorient their outlook. From my point of view, the rightness or wrongness of their separation depends entirely on *intent,* which only God can judge. For example, a wife whose alcoholic husband needs to experience life without the support of his family may find temporary separation to be the only method of forcing him to seek professional help. This crisis of loneliness may be the last hope to jar the man to his senses, and his wife could be doing a loving thing by making him more miserable! If *this* is the desire that motivates the more responsible partner to separate, then I find no scriptural condemnation of it. But please be warned! This understanding can also provide an open door to rationalization for those who are unhappy in marriage and are seeking an easy way out. I am certainly not sanctioning that maneuver.

**Q.** Since almost every couple fights from time to time, what distinguishes a *healthy* marriage in conflict from one that is in serious trouble? I'm asking how a husband and wife can know when their interpersonal struggles are within normal limits and when they are symptoms of more ominous problems.

**A.** It is true that conflict occurs in virtually all marriages. That is how resentment and frustration are ventilated. The difference between stable families and those in serious trouble reflects what the battles accomplish. In healthy relationships, a period of confrontation ends in forgiveness—in drawing together—in deeper respect and understanding—and sometimes in sexual satisfaction. But in unstable marriages a period of conflict produces greater pain and anger that persists until the next fight. When that occurs, one unresolved issue is compounded by another and another. That accumulation of resentment is an ominous circumstance in any marriage. Isn't this why the Apostle Paul admonished us not to let the sun go down on our wrath (Eph. 4:26)?

**Q.** Is it harder for a man or for a woman to recover from an affair by a spouse?

**A.** I have not observed any appreciable difference between the sexes at the time of disclosure. Both husbands and wives suffer incalculable anguish when a mate is unfaithful. Men do seem to have a cultural advantage after the crisis is over, however. Their work is a better diversion and their economic consequences are less severe. They also find it easier to find someone new, as a rule. But *no one wins* in illicit affairs of the heart.

**Q.** You referred above to a kind of "blindness" that occurs when a victim of an affair denies the truth. Mary Ann said she didn't notice her husband's infidelity because she didn't *want* to see it. I think I did the same thing when my husband was fooling around with my best friend. The affair went on for two years before I could acknowledge it to myself. But why would I deny the truth? Why do victims "choose" to be blind?

**A.** The psychological process is called *denial,* and it is designed to protect the mind from an unacceptable thought or reality. You see, once a person admits to himself that his beloved spouse has been unfaithful, then he is obligated to deal with that circumstance. The extremely painful experiences of grief, anxiety, and insomnia become inevitable once the truth has been faced. Furthermore, the injured person fears that a confrontation with the unfaithful partner might drive him into the arms of the new lover. Given these concerns, the unconscious mind apparently chooses not to notice the affair in the hope that it will blow over and be forgotten. Obviously, there is ample motivation for a vulnerable person to deny what his eyes tell him.

When the evidence of unfaithfulness becomes overwhelming, a man or woman will sometimes "ask" the guilty spouse to assist with the denial. This is done by making accusations in the hope of being proven wrong. For example, a wife will say, "Are you and Donna seeing one another?"

"No, I've told you a thousand times that nothing is going on," he lies.

"But where were you until 2:00 A.M. last night?"

"I had car trouble. Now will you get off my back?"

This wife knows her husband's story is phony, but she

continually asks him to lie to her. And interestingly, she does not feel obligated to "blow the whistle" on him until he *admits* his involvement . . . which may never happen. These tacit agreements help her maintain the illusion that "all is well."

Denial has many applications and uses in human experience. It will permit a woman to ignore a suspicious lump in her breast, or the drugs in her son's bedroom, or the debt that the family is accumulating. Through this process the mind is protected for a time, but it often permits even greater disasters to gain a foothold in our lives.

Q. How should a person respond to someone who is in denial? I have a very good friend whose wife is cheating on him, but he chooses not to see it. Should I make him face reality?

A. I am uncomfortable in giving a blanket answer to that question, in view of all the thousands of specific situations to which it could be applied. There *are* times when denial is the only link to sanity or stability, and that must be preserved. On other occasions, it can be a loving thing to break the bubble of illusion. Either way, it is risky to awaken a dreamer, as Jean discovered when she tried to inform her daughter of her father's misbehavior. The girl couldn't accept what she was hearing. If the need for denial is intense, the individual will often lash out at the one who threatens its validity.

Q. What surprises me most about the dialogue we've heard is that all four of the unfaithful spouses called themselves Christians. In fact, Jean's husband was a career churchman and a teacher in a Christian college, and Sue's husband was chairman of a "moral action committee." These were seasoned believers—not merely babes in Christ. How could they cheat on their spouses? What goes on in the mind of someone who violates his own standard of morality in so blatant a manner?

A. Like you, I'm amazed at the audacity of those who pursue affairs while calling themselves Christians. You talk about moral gymnastics! Such people can cite the Seventh Commandment by heart ("Thou shalt not commit adultery"), and they fully understand God's promise to punish sinful behavior, yet somehow they expect to break His laws with impunity! Not only is their behavior forbidden by God, but it's also in violation of every moral code in the civilized world. If that isn't heavy enough, an unfaithful spouse has to deal with the responsibility for crushing his or her wife or husband, and for warping the children of their union— those innocent and unsuspecting kids who are about to be shredded by one parent's selfishness and shame. All told, it's enough to cool off some of the most passionate playboys and playgirls. In fact, millions have come right to the door of an affair, and, having seen what lies just over the threshold, have retreated to the arms of a relieved spouse.

**Q.** It would appear to me that more Christians are involved in divorces now than ever before, and that disturbs me. Some are saying that the Bible has been misunderstood on this subject and that there *is* justification for the dissolution of marriage within Scripture. Do you agree with these reinterpretations?

**A.** Like you, I am aware of a loosening attitude toward divorce and remarriage within Christian circles and by religious leaders. There has always been pressure on those in positions of authority to "modernize" the Bible and make it seem to endorse the behaviors that make us feel guilty. But any attempt to tamper with eternal truths makes me very uneasy. For example, a recent publication by an evangelical theologian completely reversed the meaning of Jesus' teachings by providing readers with a complicated mumbo-jumbo about context and background. Lo and behold, it turns out that Jesus didn't mean it when He said, "I tell you that anyone who divorces his wife, except for marital unfaithfulness, and marries another woman commits adultery" (Matt. 19:9, NIV). This statement would have been much easier to explain away if Jesus hadn't been so explicit in His response!

Returning to your question, I do not want to sound un-charitable or dogmatic in response to the views of fellow Christians. But I admit I am concerned by what appears to be an effort to squeeze the Bible into a twentieth century mold. It just won't fit!

Q. What, then, is *your* theological position on the subject of divorce? Is remarriage ever permissible for Christians?

A. Although it is evident that I have very strong personal con-victions on that subject, I recognize my inadequacies to an-swer your question as a Biblical authority. I am not a theologian and I prefer to quote a writer who is. Therefore, I have chosen to respond to your question by quoting what my good friend, Dr. Chuck Swindoll, had to say in his book *Strike The Original Match.* I agree with the explanation he has offered therein. For purposes of brevity, I have omitted sections of his discussion and urge the reader to consult Dr. Swindoll's book for further extrapolation and Biblical support.

## DIVORCE AND REMARRIAGE: A CONTROVERSIAL SUBJECT

I'm convinced that there is no way any group of Christians picked at random would ever come to unanimity on the subject [of divorce and remarriage]. I'll go further. I don't believe a bus load of American evangelical theologians would be in unani-mous agreement on divorce and remarriage even if they toured the United States an entire summer! It's a controversial issue, for sure. Therefore, no matter what I may conclude, I am confident some very reliable, competent, and equally sincere people will disagree. So save your cards and letters!

The question everyone wants answered is this: When is divorce permissible? Because of limited time and space, I will spare you a lot of verbiage and supportive quotations. Suffice it to say, I will answer the question with remarriage in mind. In other words, my answers assume that we are really asking, "Are there any Biblical grounds for remarriage?"

I believe there are. I have searched the Scriptures, read everything I can get my hands on, and discussed this issue with my wife, my friends, fellow staff, church board members, pastors, many theological professors, and other serious students of the Bible. I have talked with numerous divorced people, single persons, married couples, publishers, authors on the subject, and authorities in the field—both Christian and non-Christian. Here are my conclusions, simplified for the sake of clarity.

I believe the Christian has Biblical grounds for remarriage when the divorce transpired under one of the three situations described as follows:

1. *When the marriage and divorce occurred prior to salvation.*

In 2 Corinthians 5:17 we read these words: "Therefore if any man is in Christ, he is a new creature; the old things passed away; behold, new things have come."

I take this literally. I even take it to the extreme! I think "new" means "new" . . . so when God promises the believing sinner that he is "a new creature," then I take that to mean exactly that. A brand new, fresh creation. Unlike before. When God promises the passing away of "old things," it surely includes divorce prior to salvation. After all, being alienated from God and at enmity with Him, how could any unbeliever possibly know His will regarding the choice of a lifetime mate? Having thought through this very carefully, I believe it falls within the context of God's superabundant grace to wipe our slate clean when we turn, by faith, to Christ the Lord.

When the marriage and divorce occurred prior to salvation, I believe God grants His "new creation" the freedom to remarry.

2. *When one's mate is guilty of sexual immorality and is unwilling to repent and live faithfully with the marriage partner.*

Much has been written on this particular issue, I realize. I repeat, I have read everything I can get my hands on, so I do not write these words hurriedly or superficially. I am fully aware of the difficulties connected with determining who is really the guilty party when it comes to sexual promiscuity. I also acknowledge the subjectivity involved in identifying "sexual immorality." Such matters must be carefully determined, usually with the help of a qualified counselor who can provide objectivity and wisdom in matters this serious. Each case must be considered independently.

Nevertheless, we cannot ignore or deny what Christ said in Matthew 19:9: "And I say to you, whoever divorces his wife, except for immorality, and marries another woman commits adultery."

All sorts of interpretations have been suggested to explain what our Lord was saying. Frankly, having examined every one of the suggestions and theories (some of them are incredibly forced and complicated), I return to the verse and accept it at face value.

Throughout my Christian life I have operated under a very simple—yet reliable—principle of interpretation: If the normal sense makes good sense, seek no other sense. Let's do that here.

When a spouse is guilty of immoral sexual conduct with another person and is unwilling to remain faithful to the innocent partner, the option is there for the faithful mate to divorce and remarry.

Before moving on to the third reason, let me ask you to reread that last sentence. I want to amplify it for a few moments. Two thoughts need to be emphasized. First, this is not simply a case of quickie sex on the sly—a one-time-only experience. This is *porneia*. I take this to mean an immorality that suggests a sustained unwillingness to remain faithful. I hesitate to use the term lest I be misinterpreted—but I think of the idea of an immoral life style, an obvious determination to practice a promiscuous relationship outside the bonds of marriage.

Second, the faithful mate has the option to leave . . . but such is not mandatory. I have seen numerous marriages rebuilt rather than ended because the faithful partner had no inner peace pursuing a divorce. How much better to look for ways to make the marriage work rather than anxiously anticipate evidence that is needed to break off the relationship. But there are occasions when every attempt has been made to keep the marriage together . . . but sustained sexual infidelity won't allow it. It is in such cases our Lord grants freedom from that miserable and unbearable bond.

3. *When one of the mates is an unbeliever and willfully and permanently deserts the believing partner.*

You probably don't need to be told that all sorts of suggestions have been made by sincere and qualified students of Scripture to explain what constitutes desertion . . . and to spell out what "not under bondage" really means. Because I promised to spare you numerous quotations and tedious pages of verbiage, I'll not attempt to represent all the opinions that range from unbelievably conservative to downright crazy (in my opinion!). But perhaps a word of caution is needed.

When we read of the departure of the unbelieving partner, obviously Paul is not referring to a temporary, quick decision to chuck it all and bail out . . . only to return in a little while. No, leaving means leaving. Permanence is definitely in mind. It implies a determined and willful decision that results in leaving the relationship with no desire to return, no interest in cultivating that home, no plan to bear the responsibilities, and no commitment to the vows once taken. That's "leaving." And the one being left has little doubt in such cases. The marriage is over. Finished. Ended.

### A Summary and a Warning

I agree with John R. W. Stott: [Divorce was] a divine concession to human weakness.* No Christian should aggressively seek the dissolution of his or her marriage bond. Some of the very best things God has to teach His children are learned while working through marital difficulties.

Endless stories could be told of how God honored the perseverance of abused and ignored partners as they refused to give up.

But in certain extreme cases, against the wishes and efforts of the committed mate, the marriage bond is destroyed beyond any human ability to restore it. Scripture teaches that God's "divine concession to human weakness" is occasionally justified, allowing

---

* John R. W. Stott, *Christian Counter-Culture* (Downers Grove, IL: Inter-Varsity Press, 1978), p. 95.

the Christian divorced person the right and freedom to remarry in the Lord.

Before closing the chapter, a warning must be sounded. Being human and sinful and weak, we are all equipped with a remarkable ability to rationalize. Unless we consciously guard against it, when we experience marital difficulties, we'll begin to search for a way out instead of a way through. Given sufficient time in the crucible, divorce will seem our only option, our long-awaited and much-deserved utopia. And we will begin to push in that direction, at times ignoring the inner voice of God's Spirit and at other times violating the written principles of God's Word. Either is a grievous act.

I warn all of us against such thought and actions. To carry out that carnal procedure is to short-circuit the better plan God has arranged for His people and, worse than that, is to twist the glorious grace of God into a guilt-relieving excuse for giving us what we have devised instead of accepting what He has designed.

Where God permits divorce and remarriage, humbly let us accept it without fear or guilt. Let us not call "unclean" what He now calls clean. But neither let us put words in His mouth and make Him say what He, in fact, has not said. No matter how miserable we may be.

There is something much worse than living with a mate in disharmony. It's living with God in disobedience.*

---

\* Taken from the book *Strike the Original Match* by Charles R. Swindoll, copyright 1980 by Multnomah Press, Portland, Oregon 97266. Used by permission.

# 12.

# *Anatomy of Adultery*

*B*ecause the previous chapters, and perhaps the entire book, have left the impression that infidelity is typically committed by self-centered males who betray their devoted wives, I feel I should present the other side of that coin. At least one secular poll reportedly found that among those under twenty-nine years of age, "significantly more married women are having affairs than married men." The same study also indicated that teenage girls lose their virginity earlier than boys, on the average. I have no way of assessing the accuracy of those conclusions, but I do know that sexual experimentation among women is becoming increasingly common today. It is apparent in the world around us.

Shirley and I used to enjoy jogging in the park near our home during early morning hours. Every day we noticed two cars parked side by side in a remote section of the lot, with one car empty and two people sitting close together in the other. The windows were always very steamy. It didn't take a detective to figure out what was going on. We surmised that these secret lovers had made their spouses think they were at work instead of kissing and cuddling in the park. Somewhere near my home are two unidentified families, and perhaps two sets of children, that unknowingly await the tragic moment of disclosure.

It has been my observation that when wives engage in extramarital sexual activity, a unique pattern of circumstances often precedes it. Women are much less likely to be involved in the multiple, casual relationships that characterized the men described in chapter 9. Instead, unfaithful women often take the pathway pursued by Mike's wife. A vulnerable lady may find herself involved in an entanglement which she neither sought nor expected. It just seemed to "happen" when she and another needy person were thrown together at the right (or wrong) time. Yet the consequences of unexpected disloyalty are just as deadly as infidelity in the first degree.

To brace my female readers against this deceptive sin, and to help their husbands avoid the precipitating circumstances, let me describe what I have called an "anatomy of adultery." It reflects the most common pathway to *female* indiscretion (though not the only one), and it can be divided into eleven distinct stages or steps. I wrote it after counseling yet another family in the throes of divorce.

## ANATOMY OF ADULTERY

*Wife's Perspective*                    *Husband's Perspective*

### STAGE 1

The wife is in a state of emotional need. She is lonely, suffers from low self-esteem, and has had difficulty making female friends. She reaches for the romantic involvement of her husband but he fails to notice. She resorts to nagging and complaining, which puts a greater wedge between them.

The husband has made business commitments that he must meet. He's in a highly competitive and satisfying position, and his emotional energies are drained by the time he comes home. He loves his wife but doesn't have much time to "carry her," psychologically.

*Wife's Perspective*

*Husband's Perspective*

## STAGE 2

She experiences greater frustration and depression, which gradually give way to anger. She begins to "bludgeon" her bewildered husband for his failures in the home.

He makes some feeble attempts to relate to his wife, especially after emotional explosions have occurred between them. But this leopard finds it difficult to change his spots. He is still overcommitted at work, whether he likes it or not, and he constantly falls back into familiar patterns.

## STAGE 3

This needy woman is now in a dangerous position. She is vulnerable to any attractive, available man who comes into her life. Inevitably, it seems, such an encounter occurs. A casual introduction to a flirtatious man sets the wheels in motion, and he quickly becomes the object of her fantasies, hopes and dreams. He appears to be so compassionate compared to her husband, so much more dignified, so much more in touch with her feelings, so much more worthy of respect. Nothing illicit has occurred at this point, but she's spending a great deal of time *thinking* about an affair with this specific man. Jesus once said, "As a man (or woman) thinketh in his heart, so is He!" Alas, this woman is becoming an adulteress in her mind.

The husband continues in ignorance of what his wife is experiencing. His mind is elsewhere. He wishes she would be happier because he *does* love her and the kids, but he has no idea how her unhappiness relates to him.

*Wife's Perspective*                    *Husband's Perspective*

## STAGE 4

An extramarital relationship gradually begins to heat up. It's no sudden romp in the grass. Rather, the affair grows slowly, with more secret meetings and an escalating friendship. She feels guilty, of course, but the excitement is incredible. Anyway, her husband doesn't seem to care. Finally it happens; a sexual experience occurs.

The man of the house is still not aware of any unfaithfulness. He may notice some coolness and a lessened demand for his attention, but his suspicions are not aroused. Her hostility to him may increase during this time, but he has already become accustomed to that attitude in her.

## STAGE 5

More illicit sexual activity now transpires, with all the guilt, fear and raw passions that accompany this way of life. Her spiritual life rapidly deteriorates, as she lies and rationalizes and lives a double standard. It is a tough assignment to play-act the role of a faithful wife when she's giving her all to someone else. Bible reading and church attendance become less frequent or even nonexistent. She loses all sexual interest in her husband.

The man may now begin to worry about the deteriorating relationship for the first time. He doesn't yet have much evidence on which to base his suspicions, but he knows intuitively that something has changed. His reaction is still one of confusion at this stage.

## STAGE 6

For the wife, the affair continues hot and heavy. Every minute that can be spent with her new lover is grabbed.

Somehow discovery occurs, usually by "accident." Perhaps a tiny lie is betrayed, or an anonymous phone call is received. His

| *Wife's Perspective* | *Husband's Perspective* |
|---|---|
| | first reaction is one of *utter* shock! He can't believe what has happened. He confronts his wife in one of the most emotional and unpleasant encounters in their lives. It will be remembered forever. |

## STAGE 7

| | |
|---|---|
| Her feelings of guilt and embarrassment are concealed behind rationalizations and recriminations against her husband. She is going to admit nothing that she doesn't have to disclose. Depending on the quality of her husband's evidence, she may continue to lie and deny at this stage. On the other hand, some women will break emotionally, weeping profusely and begging for forgiveness. Either way, this stage is characterized by wildly fluctuating emotions from day to day. | For the first time, enormous pain is felt by the husband. Whereas he could hardly give his wife the time of day a few weeks before, his unfaithful partner suddenly becomes the *only* important thing in his life. This guy who would rather go to a football game with his male friends than be with his wife—the man who hid behind the newspaper every night after work—now finds himself pleading for her favors. He crawls. He cries. He bargains. I've known men in this fix who called me from a phone booth near a freeway where they had been driving eighty miles an hour, looking for a place to crash their cars. A pitiful sight! |

## STAGE 8

| | |
|---|---|
| We come now to a critical juncture. When confronted by the spiritual implications of their be- | The pain experienced by the husband is intensified. He had never known such stress in his |

*Wife's Perspective*                    *Husband's Perspective*

havior, some women decide not to sacrifice their families, but to reconcile with their husbands. Others are determined to have their own way and go with the new lover, who is infinitely more exciting and alluring. Such a woman may pity her mate and desire not to hurt him, but she finds him boring and disdainful.

entire life. Jealousy burns through his mind as he imagines what his wife and her lover have done together. At alternating times he feels rage, guilt, remorse, love, hate, despair, etc. He makes all the mistakes described in the early chapters of this book, including appeasement, entrapment, panic, threats of violence, and self-debasement. Now *he* is dealing with the low self-esteem which his wife experienced some years ago.

*Note: Since the classic pattern can go in several directions at this point, depending on the reaction of the woman, we will follow the one where her affair continues.*

## STAGE 9

It has been said, "A woman wants a man she can look up to, but one who won't look down on her." It is true. Women need to hold their husbands in a certain awe, or at least in modest respect, if their relationship is to be healthy. The Apostle Paul instructed men to *love* their wives, but he told women to *respect* their husbands. Those are the conditions needed respectively by each sex. Nevertheless, this woman begins to experience a tug of war in her mind. The welfare of her children weighs

The agitation of stage 8 continues unabated, especially as the husband contemplates the details of what his wife and her lover are experiencing together. He doesn't think he can stand it, and that sense of panic is evident in everything he does. His work suffers and his face reveals the strain he is under. Unfortunately, the behavior now being shown by the rejected lover serves to assassinate respect and put a severe strain on a relationship already stretched to the breaking point.

*Wife's Perspective*                    *Husband's Perspective*

heavily in her thoughts, and she knows they are hurting. She sees the flaws and faults of her new lover for the first time, and the romantic dream fades just a bit. Sex with him is still exciting, but it no longer thrills her as it did. All the ugly realities of divorce stare her in the face. Is that what she wants? Still, she remembers her prior state of loneliness and low self-esteem. "I can't go back to that!" she says to herself. It is this motivation, more than any other, that may push her over the edge.

## STAGE 10

The decision to divorce is made; lawyers are consulted; papers are filed; hearings are held and property is divided. The children are caught between the parents and become the object of struggle and contest. A bloody custody battle is fought with numerous casualties on both sides. Harsh words are exchanged. Tears are shed. Then they are dried, life goes on: people learn to cope. But every now and then, just before the woman goes to sleep at night or perhaps in a moment of quietness, she

The human mind cannot tolerate agitated depression and grief indefinitely. The healthy personality will act to protect itself in time, throwing off the despair and groping for stability. One method by which this is accomplished is by turning pain into anger. Thus, the husband may harbor a deep but quiet hostility toward his wife—the one who betrayed his trust, shattered his home, took half his money and hurt his kids. He no longer accepts the blame for what has happened, feeling instead that he

*Wife's Perspective*

asks herself, "What have I done?"

*Husband's Perspective*

was betrayed. He would not take his wife back now under any circumstances. He begins to brace himself for whatever may come.

STAGE 11

As events unfold, she weds her new lover and life is exciting for a time. But eventually, it becomes more like her first marriage. The great thrill is gone, the relationship having been "too hot not to cool down." Daily living is routine once more. The dating and laughter and the walks and talks give way to doing laundry and fixing meals and going to work. The marriage may be successful or it may not. The probabilities of another divorce are higher than for first marriages, *perhaps because both partners have demonstrated a willingness to fool around with married lovers!* If there is no divorce, the new husband and wife plod on through the years, moving inexorably toward the Great Day of Accountability when their lives will be laid bare before their Maker. These two people have convinced themselves they did the right thing—except . . . when they think of the children . . . they feel guilty.

The man gradually works his way through bitterness to a state of apathy. Life returns to normal except that his wife is gone. He will probably remarry, since divorced men are in much greater demand than divorced women in our society. He again loses himself in work and slams the door on the past. Except . . . when he thinks of the kids . . . he feels guilty.

But every man is tempted, when he is drawn away of his own lust, and enticed. Then when lust hath conceived, it bringeth forth sin; and sin, when it is finished, bringeth forth death.

*James 1:14–15*, KJV

I know I've painted a very dark picture on my canvas, but it represents reality as I perceive it. Adultery is not pleasant either to read or to write about, but I feel that someone must describe the sordid side of this sin. Night after night on television we see beautiful people jumping into bed with strangers and it all looks so exciting. Popular magazines tell us that sex, lots of sex with a variety of partners, is not only healthy but everyone is doing it. Ridiculous books like *Open Marriage* make extramarital affairs sound like a tonic guaranteed to revitalize tired relationships. Alas, at times it seems like the entire world of entertainment is organized for the sole purpose of propagating that one enormous lie, and no one is effectively refuting it.

What I am about to write will sound phony but, so help me, it is true. I have secluded myself with my family to write this book, and few others know I am in this city. Nevertheless, my telephone rang immediately after I completed the paragraph above. The caller was a distressed woman asking for consultation regarding her marital problems. She told me that her husband (who claims to be a Christian believer) ran off with a young girl and is now living with her in a nearby city. There it is again—another outbreak of the epidemic that sweeps the western world. That's why I've felt compelled to write this difficult book. Infidelity and marital conflict are cancers that gnaw on the soul of mankind, twisting and warping innocent family members who can only stand and watch.

But let the record show that the guilty suffer severely, too. God has not forbidden indiscriminate sexuality just to deprive us of fun. In His ultimate wisdom, He has attempted to protect us from the devastation of sin. Herpes and syphilis and Acquired Immune Deficiency Syndrome (AIDS) and gonorrhea are not the only consequences of unbridled passion. The greater pain is experienced in the soul of mankind. Consider the following letter from Florence.

Dear Dr. Dobson:

We heard your radio program during which you discussed the consequences of adultery. This has happened in our family and we would like to share our story with you.

My husband has been unfaithful to me through the years even though I had never known or wanted any other man. Finally, his loose attitude toward the marriage began to affect my commitment, and I too got entangled in an affair. It lasted for nine months before my husband found out about my involvement. He has been devastated ever since.

Bill is experiencing such guilt and anger toward himself now, because he feels that this would never have happened if he had not been unfaithful. He says he has lost something more precious than gold when he lost this part of me. His emotions do strange things. First, he is deeply angry at me for doing this to him; then he's mad because I told him about it. His anger and hate then turn onto the other man—sometimes to the point of his wanting to do something destructive to him. At other times he goes through the mental torture of imagining what "took place" between me and the other man. This angry stage occurs about one-third of the time. Another third is spent weeping and hating himself, and a final third in loving me so much that nothing matters so long as we are together.

We've spent endless hours in prayer that God would take the anger and pain away, or help us cope with it. All we want now is to be happy and make up for what we've done to each other. We feel a greater love for one another than ever before and we want to serve the Lord throughout our remaining years together. But Bill and I need for this torment to go away! Can you help us?

Florence

Bill has discovered one of the eternal principles on which the universe is founded: we are all governed by a moral code that cannot be violated without inevitable consequences. It has been true throughout human history. In fact, Bill's remorse reminds me of the turmoil King David experienced from a similar sin more than three thousand years ago. As you will recall, David had fallen into an adulterous relationship with Bathsheba while her husband was away at war. God was very angry at the king for this sinful act and vowed that his punishment would involve rebellion and sexual indiscretion within his own family.

That curse was manifested in the life of David's son, Absalom, who tried to overthrow the king. As a deliberate insult, the defiant young man had sexual intercourse publicly with his father's wives. Civil war resulted and Absalom was executed after his hair was caught in the thistles of a tree.

When David learned of the death of his son, he knew that his own sin with Bathsheba had led to this tragic climax. His agony is described in one of the most pathetic scenes of the Bible: "And the king was much moved, and went up to the chamber over the gate, and wept: and as he went, thus he said, O my son Absalom, my son, my son Absalom! would God I had died for thee, O Absalom, my son, my son!" (2 Sam. 18:33, KJV).

What a tragic moment, as David paced the floor in guilt and regret. Adultery always produces this kind of devastation—both for the innocent spouse and for the guilty, to say nothing of the young "Absaloms" in the family. It is an inevitable law of God! Solomon, another of David's sons, said it best:

> Can a man scoop fire into his lap without his clothes being burned?
> Can a man walk on hot coals without his feet being scorched?
> So is he who sleeps with another man's wife; no one who touches her will go unpunished.
> Men do not despise a thief if he steals to satisfy his hunger when he is starving.
> Yet if he is caught, he must pay sevenfold, though it costs him all the wealth of his house.

But a man who commits adultery lacks judgment; whoever does so destroys himself.

Blows and disgrace are his lot, and his shame will never be wiped away.

*Proverbs 6:27–33*, NIV

Why have I bothered to repeat what every Christian must surely know—that sexual promiscuity is forbidden by God and is destructive to marriage? I suppose these words serve to express my own frustration at the permissiveness of the age, when we have become so blasé concerning evil in all its varieties. This disease of sin is more deadly, more virulent, than any illness known to mankind, yet the family is gripped by its fever. At a moment when the Christian church is desperately needed to call the nation to repentance, so much of its emphasis is placed on the supposed benefits of Christian "enlistment"—health, wealth and business wisdom. "Something good is going to happen to you today," we sing. Perhaps. Perhaps not.

I sit in churches and listen to this positive rhetoric that tickles our ears, while all around me are people who have been in my office at one time or another. Every form of rebellion against God is represented behind their glassy eyes, while the disease that afflicts mankind goes undiagnosed and undetected. I thank God for ministers who still have the courage to call sin by its name, and to urge their congregations toward repentance and obedience to the Lord of Hosts.

I am also thankful that *no sin* is beyond the forgiveness of God. Even the most selfish, evil sinner on the face of the earth can obtain total cleansing at the cross. All that is required is for him to repent of his sins and believe on the name of the Lord Jesus Christ. He is then baptized into the fellowship of believers. Henceforth, he is promised that his misdeeds will be separated as far as the east is from the west, and remembered against him no more throughout eternity. That is the greatest proposition ever offered in the long history of mankind.

# 13.

# *Loving Toughness in Other Settings*

Now that I've told you more than you ever wanted to know about adultery, it is time to apply the *love must be tough* philosophy to other difficult family problems. As indicated, this approach to interpersonal relationships is certainly not confined to illicit love affairs or even to the framework of marriage. It has its place wherever two or more people come into contact with one another. Let's take a brief look, then, at some of the thorny situations that confront today's families in the context of our theme, again referring to letters received in response to the "Focus on the Family" radio series.

## I. THE WIFE OF A VIOLENT SPOUSE

Dear Dr. Dobson:

This is an extremely difficult letter to write, but I must have help. My husband and I have been married for twelve years, and throughout most of this time, he has had a secret problem. Only I know that he has a violent temper that is absolutely terrifying to me. He is a leader in our church and is a very prominent lawyer in our city. Everyone respects him highly. But when he is at home he is a different person.

At least once or twice a month he explodes over something the

146

kids or I have done to irritate him, and he becomes furious. He yells, throws things, threatens me, and makes an awful scene. If I say the wrong thing or if I say *anything,* he beats me with his fists.

Last week he loosened three of my teeth and cut the inside of my lip. I really thought he was going to kill me! This happened because I failed to do some errands he asked me to get done. What bothers me is that the beatings are becoming more frequent and more violent as time goes by.

After each fight is over, my husband refuses to take any blame for what happened. He steadfastly insists that I am at fault for deliberately provoking him. He interprets everything as a personal insult. The only way I can keep him calm is to do *everything* he asks and to hold inside every thought that might make him angry.

I don't know what to do. I really do love my husband. He's a fine man when he isn't mad about something. He never shows this side of himself in public, even when he is frustrated. No one has any idea he is a wife abuser. I haven't told anyone, and my husband would blow straight up if I asked him to go with me for counseling. No telling what he'd do if he knew I was consulting *you!*

So what can I do? I don't believe in divorce. I am trying to be gentle and cautious at all times, but inevitably I step on his toes and he explodes again. I'm so tired of being beaten and then having to stay home for days to hide my bruises.

How do I deal with this situation?

Laura

The problem of wife abuse is reaching epidemic proportions in today's families. The violence that is characteristic of the culture around us is being translated into husband-wife relationships and to parent-child interactions. Entire volumes have been addressed to this problem, and I am not likely to add to that understanding in the time and space allotted here. I can, however, offer Laura a condensed answer which would be the basis for our work if I were counseling her personally.

As I see it, Laura only has four alternatives in response to her circumstance. They are:

1. *Remain silent at home, walk on cracked eggs, and be the eternal*

*conciliator.* She is taking this approach now, but it is not succeeding. No matter how passive she becomes, she will eventually trigger the anger of her uptight husband. Furthermore, she'll pay a terrible price emotionally for living on a powder keg year in and year out. For the long term, this is not the answer.

2. *Divorce her husband.* As a Christian, I agree with Laura that divorce is not the solution to this problem. Our purpose should be to change her husband's behavior, not kill the marriage.

3. *Proceed with an "emotional divorce," remaining married but keeping herself detached and independent from her husband.* This form of "emotional isolation" will shield Laura from psychological pain, but it will make for a terrible relationship. I don't favor it.

4. *The love must be tough response.* This is risky and psychologically expensive, but it is my choice and my recommendation. In essence, Laura is being emotionally blackmailed by her husband. He is saying by his behavior, "Do what I wish or I'll beat you." She must break out of that tyranny while she's still young enough to cope with the consequences. This might be accomplished by forcing the matter to a crisis. Change of behavior does not occur when waters are smooth, as we have seen; it sometimes happens after a storm. I would suggest that Laura choose the most absurd demand her husband makes, and then refuse to consent to it. Let him rage if he must rage. She should prearrange a place to go and ask friends or relatives to step in for assistance at that critical moment. Separate living quarters may be necessary until her husband settles down. He should be made to *think* that he has lost his wife over this issue, and in fact, I would recommend that she not return until there is reason to believe that he is willing to change. If that takes a year, so be it. When (and if) her husband acknowledges that he has a severe problem and promises to deal with it if she'll come home, a period of negotiations should follow. One of the conditions for reconciliation is competent Christian counseling for the psychological problem that is now apparent to every-

one but the husband. By all means, Laura will need the support of Christian friends and counselors, especially during the time of crisis. And it goes without saying that the entire matter must be bathed in prayer from the beginning. I can offer no guarantees that this advice will resolve Laura's problem with her violent husband. But I believe it represents the best possibility for success. Let me ask those of you who disagree, what would *you* advise? Counselors suggesting that this frightened woman remain passive and submissive despite the abuse should have to look into Laura's eyes and tell her that in person. I don't believe anyone should be required to live in that kind of terror, and in fact, to do so is to tolerate a behavior which could eventually prove fatal to the marriage, anyway.

*Related Question*

**Q.** Are you suggesting that *any* woman who is being beaten should take the same course of action? My husband has only hit me once in a big fight we had. Should I separate from him?

**A.** I am not offering blanket advice to every wife who has had a violent encounter with her husband. As in your case, a man can become so enraged that he does something he is immediately sorry for and would never do again. That is very different from the repetitive, pathological situation Laura is in. Let me offer another word of caution which is likely to be misunderstood by those who *want* to misunderstand. It deals with a very volatile subject that angels would fear to touch, but I feel it must be addressed. I have seen marital relationships where the woman deliberately "baited" her husband until he hit her. This is not true in *most* cases of domestic violence, but it does occur. Why, one may ask, would *any* woman want to be hit? Because females are just as capable of hatred and anger as males, and a woman can devastate a man by enticing him to strike her. It is a potent weapon. Once he has lost control and lashed out at his tormentor, she then sports undeniable evidence of his cruelty. She can show her wounds to her friends who gasp at the viciousness of that man. She can press charges against him in some cases and have him thrown in jail. She can embarrass him at his work or in the church. In short, by taking a beating, she instantly achieves a moral advantage in the eyes of neighbors, friends, and the law. It may even help her justify a divorce, or if one comes, to gain custody of her children. Remember what the Japanese sneak attack on Pearl Harbor did to American morale and unity? It solidified our forces and gave us a cause worth fighting for. There are those who believe President Roosevelt ignored warnings of the Pearl Harbor invasion for the precise purpose of unifying our resolve against a rising Japanese imperialism. In that same spirit, I have seen women belittle and berate their husbands until they set them aflame with rage. Some wives are more verbal than their husbands and can win a war of words any day of the week. Finally, the men reach a point of such frustration that they explode, doing precisely what their wives were begging them to do in the first place.

I remember one woman who came to church with a huge black eye contributed by her husband. She walked to the front of the auditorium before a crowd of five hundred people and made a routine announcement about an upcoming event. Everyone in attendance was thinking about her eye and the cad who did this to her. That was precisely what she wanted. I happened to know that her noncommunicative husband had been verbally antagonized by his wife until he finally gave her the prize she sought. Then she brought it to church to show it off. It *does* happen.

It is obvious why this analysis is inflammatory to women like Laura who are victims in the true sense of the word. They may think I am suggesting that they are responsible for their husband's violence. Not so! But domestic violence has more than one source of motivation, and that fact should be admitted.

## II. THE HUSBAND OR WIFE OF A CHILD ABUSER

My friend Paul Powers was one of the most pathetic victims of child abuse I've ever known. Both his mother and father were alcoholics who produced or adopted twelve children despite their inability to care for them. When Paul was seven years old, his mother came home from a party in a drunken stupor and collapsed before she reached the front door. The children found her the next morning lying in the snow. She contracted pneumonia and grew gravely ill. Two weeks later when Paul came home from school, his mother called him to her bedside and reached out to take his hand, but died before she could convey her thoughts. Seeing that she was gone, the child ran sobbing to his drunken father who pushed him away and began beating him with his fists. The man screamed, "Shut up! Boys don't cry like babies!" Paul's nose and two ribs were broken, and his teeth were knocked out. Even today, he bears a two-inch scar on the inside of his lower lip from the beating his father gave him that day. Paul didn't cry again until he was twenty-two years old.

That was typical of Paul's developmental years. Especially after the death of his mother, he and his siblings were subjected to cruel and vicious beatings on a regular basis. The father's abuse was reported to local authorities on numerous occasions, and each time a social worker visited the home. As soon as she had left, Paul and several of his brothers were taken to the basement, stripped, and beaten until they could not get up from the floor.

It is not surprising that Paul and every one of his eleven siblings have spent time in prison. At twelve years of age, Paul committed his first murder in a robbery attempt. He shot a female carnival worker who refused to give him her money. The judge asked Paul's father what he wanted done with the boy and he said, "Send him to hell!" Paul was confined in prison for this and related crimes and was filled with hatred and bitterness. But there in prison five years later, the most significant event in Paul's life occurred. He was seventeen years of age when he saw a Billy Graham film and began to be acquainted with the Lord Jesus Christ! Some time later he repented of his sins and was marvelously converted. Can you imagine what it must have been like for this young man who had never known love, who had experienced nothing but pain and suffering and sorrow, to be made clean and to know he was loved by the Creator Himself? His entire life was changed on that incredible day.

Paul was eventually released from prison, married a Christian woman, and became the father of a little girl. He felt God wanted him to distribute Christian films, since he had found the Lord through this medium. But times were rough. Paul and his wife were struggling to survive financially in their little ministry. It was Christmastime, and they lacked money even for groceries.

By contacting churches that had shown his films, Paul managed to collect a few dollars that were owed to him. His wife took $8.00 to the grocery store to buy food, and when she returned, he was furious to learn that she had foolishly spent $1.00 for wrapping paper and tape. While Paul and his wife argued with one another, their three-year-old daughter was quietly rummaging through the sack of groceries. When she found the wrapping paper, she took it into the living room and used it to cover a shoe box.

Paul finally realized the child was gone and went looking for her. He found her sitting on the floor with the box covered by crooked paper and half a roll of tape. When Paul saw that the child had wasted the valuable materials, his temper blew again. He resorted to the behavior he had seen as a child, grabbing the toddler by one arm and flailing her violently. Then he sent her sobbing to her room, literally terrorized. He cannot talk about the event today without crying.

The next day when gifts were exchanged, the little girl ran behind the tree and retrieved her gold box. She handed it to Paul and said, "Daddy, this is for you!" He was embarrassed that he had spanked her unmercifully for something she perceived as a gift. He slowly began unwrapping the paper and lifted the lid to find the box completely empty.

Paul's anger flared once more and he said, "What have you done? There's nothing in this box. Why did you give me an empty box? When you give someone a present you're supposed to put a gift inside it!"

The three-year-old looked up at her father innocently and said, "Oh, no, Daddy. The box is not empty! It is full of love and kisses for you. I stood there and blew kisses in there for my daddy and I put love in there too. And it is for you!"

Paul was broken. He wrapped his arms around his little girl and begged her to forgive him. Then he got on his knees before the Lord, repenting and pleading for God to purge the violent temper he had learned as a child. Never again did this remarkable man abuse any of his sons or daughters. He kept that gold box beside his bed for years, and whenever he would be hurt or discouraged, he would reach into the box and lift out an imaginary kiss from his child. Then he would place it on his cheek and say, "Thank you, Lord."

I must share a more recent chapter in Paul's story which also moved me to tears. Paul and his father had gone their separate ways in 1956 and rarely saw each other in the two decades that followed. All of Paul's attempts to make contact had been rejected. Then one day, Paul received a call from his father, who was at the Union Train Station in their town, asking if Paul could come see him. He said he would be there for only one hour. Paul and his wife jumped into the car and drove through rush hour traffic to get to the station on time. They arrived just three minutes before the train was to leave. Paul climbed aboard the train, wondering what he would say to the old man. They had been mortal enemies when they last parted company. Paul searched frantically for his father, and when they saw each other, they paused and then embraced affectionately. For the first time in his life, this 79-year-old man told his boy that he loved him. The conductor then shouted,

"All aboard!" and Paul had to hurry from the train. They had only time enough to agree that they would meet soon in a nearby city.

Paul got off the train in a state of shock. His father had *never* hugged him in his life, and in fact, had seemed totally incapable of love. "But more than that," Paul told his wife, "there was a different look about him! I saw it in his eyes. He was not the same man! I can't explain it, but that man is different!" He anticipated the time when they could talk leisurely and heal the wounds they had inflicted on one another in earlier years.

Unfortunately, the rendezvous was never held because the old man suffered a heart attack and died the following Monday. As with his mother so many years before, Paul was deprived of his father's last words. But a local pastor filled in the details at the funeral. Paul's father had indeed experienced an encounter with Jesus Christ, and had become a born-again Christian in the closing months of his life. In fact, his train journey had been a last desperate attempt to reach out to several of his children and reestablish relationships that had been ruptured for years.

I have shared Paul's story in this context for two reasons. First, because it touched me deeply and will, I know, be inspirational to others. Languishing in prison for the crime of murder, aware that no one had ever loved or needed him in his life, this young man came face to face with the compassion of God! Instead of being condemned for his sins and crimes, he was given an unconditional pardon and the record was obliterated. That is thrilling to me because I also experienced that incredible forgiveness!

But Paul's background will also help us understand the problem of child abuse. His case is characteristic of the majority of offenders today who also experienced abusive childhoods. We parents develop our child-rearing styles primarily from watching our own mothers and fathers who served as role models. Even when we disliked what they did to us, we were influenced by the standard they set. "This is how the job is done," they seemed to say. Thus, when we are grown and have children of our own, our tendency during times of frustration and stress is to imitate what we learned at home. More than 60 percent of abusive parents were themselves abused as children; that's why they need our love and understanding, not our condemnation.

Even though we understand its cause, child abuse cannot be tolerated. Its effect on a developing youngster can be devastating. That's why I recommend loving toughness when one parent observes consistent violence being inflicted on a boy or girl by the spouse. Of course, I could list an entire page of qualifiers behind that statement. What one permissive parent may interpret as child abuse may be, in fact, good discipline by the other spouse. The ideal approach is for mothers and fathers who disagree on techniques of discipline to discuss the matter with a wise, neutral counselor who can mediate the conflict.

But let's be realistic. There are hundreds of thousands of homes today where one parent is aware of injustice and cruelty on the part of the other. Perhaps the father overreacts in response to routine childishness, beating the kids in anger or vindictiveness. Or maybe a mother is thrashing a colicky infant or punishing an older child too severely. What is a concerned parent to do under those circumstances? If he goes to the authorities, he threatens to destroy his home and incur the wrath of his spouse. Furthermore, the family's reputation in the community will be tarnished and their friendships undermined. Often, the price is too great and the mother or father chooses not to pay it. Therefore, their little children suffer the brunt of this injustice without advocacy.

Worse yet, I have become aware in recent years that many mothers knowingly permit their husbands to abuse their daughters sexually for the same reasons! I have seen numerous situations where a little girl was expected to relieve the sexual pressure on her mother by satisfying the father's passions. Unbelievable, you say! Hardly! It is estimated that 20 to 25 percent of all females in this country were sexually abused as children, most of them in their own homes. I have talked to these individuals after they've grown to be women. Virtually every one of them bears scars that will never be healed. They feel utter disgust and revulsion, not for their fathers, but for *themselves!* "I feel so dirty!" is the typical comment. It is as though they have taken the entire blame for the exploitation they suffered.

Mothers and fathers, if this is going on in your home, you simply *must* come to the rescue of your child! You can't deny it another day. Nothing can make it right. Even at the risk of damaging or destroying your marriage, that little girl or boy who is being subjected to sexual exploitation or physical violence must be protected. Every child deserves a chance to grow up with a healthy mind and body. I urge you to seek professional help, today. If you don't know who to consult, talk to your pediatrician or call the toll-free Childhelp hotline to talk anonymously to a counselor. They will direct you to a local agency that can help you. Their numbers are 1–800–422–4453 and 1–800–4ACHILD. If all else fails and the abuse continues, get the child out of the house in which it is occurring. That is loving toughness under fire! Then let the Lord lead as you seek to reconcile and heal your marriage.

Finally, if *you* are the abuser, don't wait another day to seek professional consultation. Most cities have organizations that help parents with this problem. Sure, it will be painful to admit that you have hurt your children, but if you'll act now, there may still be time for your son or daughter to recover and live a normal life during the critical developmental years. You will never regret dealing with this terrible problem before it is too late. Don't be like Paul Powers's father who was in his final days on earth before showing love to his son. The same Lord who touched his life wants to do a miracle in yours, too.

## III. Wife in Financial Stress

Q. What do you say to the woman who tolerates infidelity in her husband because she has no financial resources? What if she is afraid to confront him because he could leave her in poverty?

A. I have no simple answers for that lady. Life can place us between rocks and hard places where problems seem almost unsolvable! Such is the plight of mothers raising children with little or no financial help from their ex-husbands. According to the Department of Health and Human Services, this is *the* primary source of poverty in America today. Almost half of all people living below the poverty line are divorced women with children, according to the 1980 census. The same survey revealed that half of the divorced mothers do not receive the court-ordered amount of child support from their ex-husbands. I must say that I don't understand the laissez-faire enforcement of the law in this regard. Oh, I know the courts instruct men to do their duty, but little is done to prod those who resist. In a society that is regulated to death with laws and ordinances for virtually every human activity, it does seem that we could put the squeeze on men who won't care for their kids. Even in the administration of justice, you see, *love must be tough.*

Millions of divorced men *do* pay child support, of course, and many exceed the minimum amount established by the courts. Let me share an encouraging letter I received recently from a mother who faced the problem described in the question above, but overcame it with prayer.

Dear Dr. Dobson:

I have appreciated your broadcasts this week on the subject *love must be tough.*

I am going through the very situation you talked about, an unfaithful husband after fifteen years of what I thought was a good marriage. Yes, I experienced all the emotions you mentioned plus one that I think many women face. My problem was financial insecurity.

You see, I never had worked outside the home and I was scared about how I would manage to pay the bills. It costs so much to keep kids in clothes and all the other needs today. My husband works for a Ford dealership and he's made a decent living, but we've never been able to save any money.

My husband was unfaithful and I was miserable, but because of this fear, I never confronted him with it. Finally I just confessed this fear to the Lord and told Him I was depending upon him for my finances and security. Praise the Lord, He worked it out beautifully!

I told my husband to either straighten up or leave. Well, he left, but he decided to continue with the same financial arrangements as before. Sure it hurts, but not like before when I knew he was with someone else and playing games with my emotions.

Since I confronted him with this, I have evidently taken the fun out of his relationship with this woman. I honestly believe he enjoyed the secretiveness of playing around. He treats me better now than he has for years.

The Bible says that God will make even our enemies to be at peace with us when we obey Him. This has certainly been true in my case.

Your advice is correct. The only thing I would add is for the person to ask God to give him the courage and strength to carry it out. I put up with infidelity for nine years because I didn't have that confidence.

God bless you,
Marvella

Thank you, Marvella. *Your* advice is correct, also.

## IV. Husband of a "New Woman"

Since the so-called "women's movement" has been a major force in western thought for almost two decades, it is now possible to evaluate its effect on the self-concept of women and on their marriages. Despite many concerns I have expressed in the past, the picture definitely has its positive elements. There is no doubt in my mind that the movement has brought greater respect and dignity for females, especially in the business world.

Prior to 1965, it was not uncommon for an attractive young woman in the work force to be treated like a piece of flesh, a toy to be used by men. Sexual innuendos spoken about her and within her hearing were almost expected as proof of male virility. That disrespect, and other forms of it, still occur in everyday life, but it is less common today and women know that they are entitled to better treatment. In this and many related ways, the elevated self-concept of women has been a healthy phenomenon in our culture.

But there have been casualties, too, especially when the philosophy of radical feminism is adopted uncritically by former traditionalists. I'm referring to the role reversal and change in lifestyle that often occurs when a loving wife and mother suddenly becomes a "new woman." You've seen it happen—probably within your circle of friends. One day she is raising a family, maintaining a home, doing her best to live on a budget, undergirding her husband in his career, helping out at the church or the PTA or the hospital, and trying to serve God to the best of her ability. Then overnight, or so it would seem, she makes a 90-degree turn and becomes somebody else.

Her new attitude can best be described as deeply angry. She is tired of being abused and taken for granted and disrespected. From now on, you'd better believe, she is not going to be pushed by anyone. Her new system of values has been programmed for her by feminist organizations and publications, almost as though a computer software package were keypunched into her brain. From that day forward, her primary concern is *herself!* The children will make it fine, she feels, with far less mothering. Her own career becomes all-consuming to her, and if it conflicts with her husband's work, then he'll just have to compromise. She bristles when her new beliefs are challenged or contradicted. These very words I'm writing, in fact, would make her furious. Her attitude toward God is likely to be revised too. If He's not an anti-feminist, then in her opinion, most of His people are. She just may throw overboard everything she believed before her rebirth as a "new woman."

The saddest chapter in the life of the new woman occurs when she runs—runs from her children—runs to establish a new identity—runs to the arms of another man. I remember one young woman whom I had watched with interest during her childhood and adolescence. I saw her as a high school homecoming queen, as a college coed, as a bride, and then as a mother. But the babies came too fast for her. She couldn't handle the stresses of raising toddlers and changing diapers and wiping runny noses. I'll never forget the look in her eyes when she told me, "They're driving me crazy!" But I underestimated her frustration until the day she disappeared. She left behind three beautiful kids and a bewildered, wounded husband. Her behavior changed, her faith evaporated, her morals crumbled and her former loves perished. And five people in that little family will never be the same.

What should the husband of a "new woman" do? How can he deal with her anger and spiritual rebellion? Again, at the risk of providing simplistic answers to extremely complex questions, let me list some approaches that have succeeded with others:

1. First, this hostile woman may have (and most certainly *does* have) some legitimate complaints that should be addressed. The loving part of our prescription (*love must be tough*) dictates that these irritants be given a full hearing. There will undoubtedly be places for compromise and compassion and concern. It is even possible that a man who is willing to listen to his wife may prevent the "new woman" transformation from occurring.

2. Once the storm begins to howl, it resembles the turmoil of adolescence. By that I mean that the great anger of those years will not continue at the same level of intensity forever but will dissipate in time. Until then, the purpose of the more responsible party is to get through the crisis without killing relationships and crushing families.

3. The particularly hostile "new woman" needs space during her discontent, and it should be given to her. If she would

separate from her family, let her go. If she doesn't call, leave her to her solitude. Let her feel that she is free, in the spirit I have described. Open the door to her domestic cage, but make *her* do the flying. As a responsible and faithful husband in this context, I would not voluntarily leave the family to accommodate her. If she obtains a court order to force my departure, then the responsibility rests on her shoulders.

4. At some point, especially if infidelity is involved, it will be appropriate to apply the principles of loving toughness described herein. Great wisdom and tact are required to know how and when to say, "That's enough; now make your choice. I'll accept either decision."

5. Pray consistently and seek the best counsel available.


## V. WIFE OF A HOMOSEXUAL

Dear Dr. Dobson:

I am plagued by a problem with a thousand things that worry me. It scares me half to death. My husband and I have been married for twelve years, and I've known for the past eight that he is a practicing homosexual. We have one little girl but she was kind of a miracle. We rarely have sexual relations. He has no interest in me, he says.

Warren told me he's known he was gay since he was nineteen years old and now he's thirty-eight. He was raised in an alcoholic's home, and I guess his childhood was pretty rough. I didn't know about his problem before I married him or else I never would have. Now it is terrible living with him. I never know when he's out with a guy. He works as a dancer here in Vegas, and he gets off at 2:00 A.M. But he doesn't come home until dawn. Whenever I ask where he went after work he gives me some phony story.

I am not a nagging wife but I've about reached my limit. I usually find out later that Warren has lied to me and he's been out with a man again. I believe that's all he cares about. A counselor told me that homosexuals are very self-centered people who think mainly of themselves. Even in their sexual activities, their main purpose is to please themselves. I can see that in our intimate times together, too.

I'll tell you what really scares me now. I'm starting to really not care for him anymore. Even when I learn he's made love to a guy, I just feel nothing. It happens so often that I have come to expect it. What I really want now is a divorce and I want to know if I have a right to get one on scriptural grounds. I've heard so many answers to that question from Christians I've talked to, but in watching your films, I thought you seemed like the kind of person who understands different situations and how to handle them.

I just don't know which way to turn. I want the kind of family that God describes in the Bible. I don't think my husband has a right to continue in the gay life and then stay married to me. Does he? Thank you for helping me.

Vickie

My heart goes out to you, Vickie. If there is anything more painful than knowing your mate has had an affair, it is the awareness that your spouse is involved in a gay lifestyle. I don't blame you for feeling betrayed by the man who promised to "love and cherish" you for life.

As to whether you have scriptural grounds for a divorce, I believe you do. Keep in mind that I am *not* a theologian and there are great differences of opinion on the interpretation of Scripture. You've already heard those conflicting viewpoints from your Christian counselors. But I see *no* differences between heterosexual unfaithfulness and the homosexual variety. They both are condemned in the Bible and should be considered in the same classification, morally. It is difficult to miss the intent of inspired writers who described a time when men would "burn with lust" for one another. Homosexuality is always included in lists of the most heinous sins, as seen in the following Scriptures.

Don't you know that the wicked will not inherit the kingdom of God? Do not be deceived: Neither the sexually immoral nor idolaters nor adulterers nor male prostitutes nor homosexual offenders nor thieves nor the greedy nor drunkards nor slanderers nor swindlers will inherit the kingdom of God.

*1 Corinthians 6:9–10,* NIV

Because of this, God gave them over to shameful lusts. Even their women exchanged natural relations for unnatural ones. In the same way the men also abandoned natural relations with women and were inflamed with lust for one another. Men committed indecent acts with other men, and received in themselves the due penalty for their perversion.

*Romans 1:26–27,* NIV

God in His wisdom would not have condemned this perversion if it had represented just another lifestyle chosen by gays. (A further discussion appears in the next section).

On the other hand, Vickie, I can't say that God wants you to divorce your husband. He loves Warren as much as he does you and me, and He would much rather help him turn from his sin. He would also like to heal your marriage if you and Warren will permit Him to do so. We must always distinguish between the sin—*any* sin—which God hates, and the sinner, whom He loves!

My advice to you, therefore, is that you apply the recommendations offered throughout this book. Prayerfully establish a point of crisis with Warren, and force him to choose between good and evil—between committed love and a life of homosexuality. If he wants to preserve his relationship with you, then he will need competent counseling to cope with his problem. And contrary to what you've heard, homosexuality *can* be treated successfully when the individual desperately wants to change. It isn't easy to conquer, but the majority of gays can become comfortable and reasonably satisfied in an exclusively heterosexual world.

I pray that Warren will be one of those fortunate people, with the help of God.

## CAUTION: SENSITIVE INFORMATION FOLLOWS

I permitted a friend to read a preliminary draft of this book, and he said he felt my discussion of homosexuality was inadequate. He asked me to describe the gay lifestyle for those who are not informed. Reluctantly, I agreed to do so.

If you have a weak stomach or don't wish to know the more unpleasant facts about homosexuality, I encourage you to skip the remainder of this section. The description I'm about to write will be very disturbing to most of my readers. My purpose is not to shock, but to dispel a carefully constructed myth. I repeat—don't read if you don't want to know!

Gay propaganda would have us see homosexuality as just another lifestyle being very similar to that of heterosexuals. They picture two young men or women holding hands and strolling serenely through the park, as though their perversion were merely another expression of human love. Unfortunately, the actual gay experience is another matter! It can be incredibly sordid and perverse in its most extreme context.

According to Dr. Paul Cameron, Chairperson of the Institute for the Scientific Investigation of Sexuality, homosexuality has become a major health hazard in the Western world. Whereas heterosexuals typically engage each other one on one, many homosexuals (but not all) prefer a group experience. Their orgies occur in "Gay Baths," among other places, made legal by antisodomy laws struck down by the courts in recent years. There are between 200 and 400 of these so-called bathhouses in existence in the U.S. today. (The success of these businesses has been severely affected by the AIDS phenomenon, but they are still in operation at the date of this writing.)

If you were to follow a gay man into such an establishment, this is what you would typically observe: For the next hour and a half, that individual would have oral-anal contact with ten to thirty partners, ingesting small amounts of fecal matter from each one; he would have oral-genital sex with five to ten more; he would be penetrated orally by five to ten men and would be the object of oral-genital contact by the same number. These men would all swallow fecal matter from one another, passed around from anus to genitalia to mouth to anus, etc. This is no exaggeration or overstatement. According to the second Kinsey Survey conducted in San Francisco, 83 percent of homosexuals report they practice oral-anal sex. The Gay Report, written for and by homosexuals, places the incidence at 89 percent. Likewise, 23 percent admit they routinely urinate on one another during their sexual encounters. There are other activities and characteristics of this "alternate lifestyle" that I would not even write in a frank discussion of this nature! That is the gay experience when expressed at its worst. The accuracy of this description was reviewed and verified by my friend Dr. Donald Tweedie, a Christian psychotherapist who has specialized for twenty-five years in the treatment of homosexual patients. Not all gays and lesbians participate in bathhouse behavior, of course, but according to Dr. Tweedie, even those who claim to be committed to monogamous relationships are often promiscuous. In other words, homosexual encounters with *multiple* partners are common, even for those who reject the orgiastic activities I have described.

Is it any wonder that so many homosexuals have hepatitis and other diseases? It certainly appears to explain the recent discovery of the incurable illness called AIDS, mentioned earlier, which is spreading unchecked through the gay community. According to the Center for Disease Control in Atlanta, Georgia, 100 percent of all patients diagnosed with the classical symptoms of AIDS in 1980 or before are now dead, and the number is doubling every six months. These developments carry ominous implications for the health of the nation, since homosexuals can be found in every profession and occupation. They drill our teeth, perform our surgeries, serve our food, teach our children, and provide their blood for our hospitals. Any major health hazard affecting up to ten percent of the population must be considered relevant to the totality. Yet our government is busily banning cyclamates and saccharin and ignoring the more obvious dangers that are politically volatile.

I have chosen to offer this graphic description of homosexuality not only to set the record straight, but to explain my understanding of the Biblical perspective on this lifestyle. It seems unreasonable to think that God, in His infinite wisdom, would forbid premarital or extramarital sex between a man and woman, but then wink approvingly at homosexual orgies and perversions. What nonsense! To the churches that have whitewashed the gay experience and absolved it of divine sanction, I can only say I'm glad I won't be the one to explain that stance on the Great Judgment Day!

I'll conclude this statement by repeating what I said earlier concerning the homosexual *himself* as opposed to his problem:

> I believe our obligation is to despise the sin but love the sinner. Many men and women who experience homosexual passions have not sought their way of life; it occurred for reasons which they can neither recall nor explain. Some were victims of early traumatic sexual encounters by adults who exploited them. I remember one homosexual teenager whose drunken father forced him to sleep with his mother after a wild New Year's Eve party. His disgust for heterosexual sex was easy to trace. Such individuals need acceptance and love from the Christian community, as they seek to redirect their impulses."*

## VI. HUSBAND OR WIFE OF AN ALCOHOLIC

A government survey form was reportedly sent to the president of a small company and asked, "How many employees do you have, broken down by sex?" He replied, "None that I know of. Our big problem here is alcohol."

Since we are dealing in rapid succession with *the* most difficult

---

* *Dr. Dobson Answers Your Questions* (Wheaton, IL: Tyndale House Publishers, 1982), p. 452.

marital crises facing us today, we must not fail to address the pervasive problem of alcoholism. One out of every three Americans is a close family member of an alcoholic, and the incidence seems to be rising. It is not a white man's disease or a black man's problem or an Indian weakness. It is a *human* condition, affecting all races, nationalities, and both sexes. The French, who pride themselves in their low rate of alcoholism, have a higher incidence of cirrhosis of the liver than any country in the world. Mother Russia has 22 million alcoholics among its citizens. Problem drinkers can be found among Protestants, Catholics and Jews. Some are down-and-outers, sprawled on skid-row streets; others have been at the pinnacle of public popularity and power, such as Betty Ford, Sid Caesar, Senators Wilbur Mills and Harold Hughes. We rub elbows every day with people whose lives are dominated by the bottle, the flask and the glass.

The saddest dimension of alcoholism is its effects on innocent family members, especially children who are too young to understand what is happening to their parents. The National Institute on Alcohol and Alcohol Abuse estimates that half of the problem drinkers in this country are women, many being "closet alcoholics" who successfully hide their addiction behind the doors of their homes. But they can't hide it from their kids. I shudder to contemplate how many toddlers will wander aimlessly through their homes today wondering why mommy "sleeps" so long on the floor. How many kids like little Paul Powers will be unjustly punished or made to go hungry or otherwise abused by a parent who is too drunk to care? It is difficult to overestimate the effect of alcoholism on the stability of today's families.

In the view of the vastness of this problem, I felt it should be given more than cursory attention here. Thus, I invited four authorities to my office to give us an up-to-date look at alcoholism and current methods of treatment. Included were a physician, Dr. Keith Simpson, who is past president of the National Council on Alcoholism, and Jerry Butler, a marriage, family and child therapist with twenty-five years of counseling experience. Jerry's own father committed suicide during one of his drunken binges. Also with me were "Bob," a recovered alcoholic, and his wife "Pauline," who preferred that we withhold their real names.

I did not ask these four individuals for a detailed analysis of the *problem;* we already know how serious it is. Rather, I wanted them to provide us with practical suggestions as to how family members can recognize the disease and then how they can help. The answers they gave were recorded, and are most encouraging and enlightening. (A copy of the 90-minute cassette tape, entitled "Help for the Alcoholic," is available from Focus on the Family, Box 500, Arcadia, CA 91006).

Dr. Simpson was asked whether alcoholism can be treated successfully, today. Is it a hopeless condition, or is there a way out for the victim and his family? I'll let the physician speak for himself.

"I specialized in the field of internal medicine for many years, but found it to be depressing work. I could help my patients with chronic lung disease and severe diabetes and heart disease, but in reality, my efforts were just a delaying action. Over time, the conditions worsened and the diseases progressed. I made my rounds in intensive care each day and watched people losing their battle for life, whereas my alcoholic patients were getting well. That's why I deal almost exclusively with alcoholics now and find it to be extremely rewarding work. I see people who come in with more horrible problems than you can imagine, but they get into a recovery program and in a few months, the difference is like going from night to day. So yes, not only is alcoholism treatable, but the medical community does better with this disorder than any other chronic disease. Alcoholics emerge from treatment programs more functionally integrated, more capable and more effective than before they 'caught' the disease."

That was the theme of the entire discussion: there is *hope* for the alcoholic! But before treatment can occur, the problem has to be identified and acknowledged. Toward that end, I asked

Dr. Simpson to describe the early characteristics of the disease for family members who need to be able to recognize the symptoms. Here is his reply.

"The first red flag is a 'tolerance' to alcohol. The person finds he has to drink more to achieve the same result. He calls this being able to 'hold his liquor'—a status symbol around the world. In reality, it is a danger signal indicating that a chemical adjustment has been made. Secondly, the person reaches a place where he doesn't want to talk about his drinking anymore. He knows he is consuming more alcohol than other people and he wants to avoid all reference to it. This begins a process of denial that may be with him for years to come. Thirdly, the person begins to experience blackouts. By that I mean that he has brief periods of amnesia that lengthen as time goes by. What is happening is that the brain's recording cells aren't remembering what is being said and done. Furthermore, it's a low dose phenomenon: It happens after one or two drinks. I'm not referring to the process of becoming stone drunk from the anesthetic effect of great quantities of alcohol. Instead, the person thinks back on the previous night and says, 'Gee! I can't remember a doggone thing after the second drink.' It's a scarey experience. Fourthly, the person begins to notice that he can't consistently predict how much he's going to drink once he starts. To me, this is the key feature of alcoholism and constitutes the definition of the disease. It occurs when an individual is constantly drinking more than he intended because he can't help it. He sits down to have a beer and wakes up the next afternoon. It may be hard for people to believe, but alcoholics don't intend to get drunk. They merely want to have a drink or two. That's why they can swear they'll never get drunk again, and *mean* it. They have no intention of breaking that promise. Nevertheless, they sit down to have a drink with a friend and bingo, it's morning."

At this point in our discussion, we heard from Pauline as she agreed with Dr. Simpson.

"I couldn't count the times Bob promised he would never drink again. That must be the most frustrating part of the experience—

having Bob look me straight in the eye and tell me he's through— really done with binging. He'd say, 'I've seen how it hurts you and the kids and I've had it. I promise you that I'll never do it again!' Then in a day or two he was dead-drunk. I thought he was lying to me. How could he love me and lie so many times to my face? But he wasn't lying. He *couldn't* keep his promise. Bob thought he could whip this problem with willpower, but you can't conquer a physiological problem with willpower. It's like trying to stop diarrhea by making up your mind to do so."

We asked Bob to express what he was feeling during this time of repeated failure. He said he was confused by his inability to overcome his habit.

"I thought the problem might be vodka, so I switched to scotch, and then bourbon. Then I tried meditation. Nothing worked. I tried a dozen approaches to control my drinking, but I always went back to it. Then I tried covering it up. I carried a bottle of Binaca in my pocket and always had a green tongue. I drank for six months without Pauline ever knowing it. Every Saturday morning she would wash her hair and then sit under a noisy dryer for a half hour. I could hardly wait for her to get preoccupied because I had a fifth of vodka in the cupboard. I would race in and get a can of Fresca from the refrigerator, pour half of it down the drain, and fill the other half with my vodka. Then I'd drink it in front of the television set with a halo around my head. You really have to be calculating to hide a drinking problem from those you live with. This went on for months. You see, I was addicted to a drug and was completely unaware of it."

I'm sure this pattern sounds familiar to many of my readers who live with an alcoholic. The critical question is, what can they do to help? Let's begin by describing the harmful approaches to avoid, and then we'll consider the recommendations of our panel.

1. Do not nag, complain, scream, cry, beg, plead, embarrass, label or berate the victim. He has a *disease* which he can't control. It is not within his power to overcome it alone.

2. Do not keep the alcoholic's life together by lying to his boss, covering for his irresponsibilities, bailing him out of jail and paying his bills. Such a rescuer is called an *enabler,* and he may actually prolong and worsen the problem.

3. Though opinions differ, most authorities do not look on alcoholism as a character weakness or a moral problem. It *was* a moral problem during earlier days when the person *chose* to drink excessively. But later, it was not his desire to hurt his family, stay in a drunken stupor, waste his money, etc. The alcoholic has long since lost his capacity for voluntary action.

4. Do not perpetuate the alcoholic's problem for your own selfish reasons. It is not uncommon for family members to resist any treatment for what may be unconscious motives. For example, a woman whose husband is usually drunk has *power* over her family. She is the unrivaled boss—the one who controls the money and makes all the family's decisions. As her alcoholic husband begins to recover, she may realize she is losing that power and move to sabotage his rehabilitation. Guard against these subtle forces that may undermine recovery in your homes.

We come now to the most important part of our discussion. What can family members do to help themselves and their addicted loved ones? First, it is virtually impossible to resolve this problem without outside help. In a very real sense, the entire family shares the sickness of the alcoholic. They are affected by rage, depression, disillusionment, despair, financial fear, denial, low self-esteem and myriad other emotions that accompany this illness. They are wounded in spirit and need the loving concern of those who have been there. As Jerry Butler said, "If the alcoholic does manage to recover, he is almost certain to regress unless his family has been treated, too."

But where can that outside assistance be found? Our panel was unanimous in their recommendations of Alanon, a support program for the families of alcoholics. Pauline credits them with saving her family and perhaps her life. She said, "After refusing to attend for a year I went to Alanon in desperation and finally began to get the answers I needed. I'll never forget the first night. They gave no sympathy and no advice. They just shared their experience, their strength and their hope. I latched onto it with everything I had and within a few weeks, things began to change for me. Alanon directed me toward God and helped me get my eyes off myself and on Him. Then they taught me how to deal with Bob."

I asked Bob what changes he began to notice at home and he was emphatic in his reply.

"If you really want to mess up an alcoholic's drinking fun, just get his spouse involved in Alanon. Pauline changed her approach in three ways and it bugged me like crazy: (1) Whereas she previously poured my booze down the drain, she stopped doing that or anything else to keep me from drinking. I really wondered if she loved me anymore. (2) On Mondays, I would ask her to call the office and tell them that I had the flu. She had always done that for me. But after going to Alanon, she would simply smile and say, 'No, you'll have to do that yourself.' (3) She seemed to be calmer, more in control. Before, I would come home from drinking with the guys and look for an excuse to leave again. All I had to do was pick a fight with Pauline and then say, 'All right, if that's the way you're gonna act, I'll just take off.' Now, she gets in this Alanon thing and instead of trying to hold me at home, she smiles and says, 'So long. I'm going to a meeting.' "

Getting help for the family is only the first step in recovery, of course. The second stage is tougher. How on earth can husbands or wives of problem drinkers get them to Alcoholics Anonymous or to a similar treatment program? That person is steeped in denial and his thought processes are blurred by booze. You simply can't expect him to make a rational decision, even to save his life. Begging him to cooperate is equally nonproductive. Are we blocked, therefore? Do we come down to the old, insurmountable barrier that has stood for centuries—the unwillingness of the alcoholic to seek help? No, not according to our panel.

Jerry Butler made it clear that there is a way around the resistance of the drinker. In fact, if you wait until he admits his need for help, he'll be dead first. Thousands die every year while denying they have a problem. That's why Alanon teaches family members how to confront in love. They learn how to remove the support systems that prop up the disease and permit it to thrive. They are shown how and when to impose ultimatums that force the alcoholic to admit his need for help. And sometimes, they recommend separation until the victim is so miserable that his denial will no longer hold up. In essence, Alanon teaches its own version of the *love must be tough* philosophy to family members who must implement it.

I asked Bob if he was forced to attend Alcoholics Anonymous—the program that put him on the road to recovery. He said,

"Let me put it this way. No one goes to AA just because they've got nothing better to do that evening. Everyone there has been forced to attend initially. You just don't say, 'On Monday night we watched a football game and on Tuesday we went to the movies. So what do you do on Wednesday? How about going over to an AA meeting?' It doesn't work that way. Yes, I was forced—forced by my own misery. Pauline allowed me to be miserable for my own good. It was loving duress that moved me to attend."

Though it may sound easy to achieve, the loving confrontation that brought Bob to his senses was a delicate maneuver. I must reemphasize that families should not attempt to implement it on their own initiative. Without the training and assistance of professional support groups, that encounter could degenerate into a hateful, vindictive, name-calling battle that would serve only to solidify the drinker's position. My purpose, therefore, has been to introduce my readers to the philosophy of loving toughness as applied to alcoholism, and to direct them to the organizations that will fill in the details.

Alanon Family Groups and Alcoholics Anonymous are both listed in local phone books. Also to be found there is the number of the Council on Alcoholism, which can provide further guidance. Finally, there are neighborhood or regional alcoholism programs provided by hospitals, governmental agencies and private organizations. They can help you. Most will not assault your faith as a Christian, and in fact, may well strengthen your dependence on God.

If you or a family member is struggling with the disease of alcoholism, you do not have to fight it alone. Call for help today.

## VII. Daughter of an Alcoholic

Dear Dr. Dobson:

Hi. My name is Karen and I am fourteen years old. I really enjoy your radio programs. I thought it was sad when you talked about your father. My dad and I don't get along so well. He used to be a policeman but not any more. He lost his job because he is an alcoholic. He's been to doctors and he's so far gone he can't be helped.

Dad always gets drunk and takes out his problems on the rest of the family. He's always sitting in taverns, somewhere. Living with an alcoholic is like living in hell. One night I was talking to a friend next door on the telephone and my dad heard me. He had come home drunk as usual. He came to my door, threw it open and yelled, "If you don't get off that phone I'm going to kill you." I knew he meant it.

I hung up the phone and sneaked out the back door. I went to a friend's house and spent the night there. Then I came home and crawled in a window at 6:00 A.M. so no one would notice I was gone. I was really scared.

I hate living with an alcoholic. I get very angry at my dad. I've had to put up with his drinking since I was born. I always have problems at home. Please help me!

Karen

I feel your pain, Karen, and I have some advice that will help you. First, your father is *not* too far gone. He can still be helped. There are no hopeless alcoholics—just alcoholics without hope. I'm sure your dad hates what he has become even more than you do, but he doesn't know how to overcome the disease he has.

Believe it or not, you can help him. Listed in your phone book is an organization called Alateen. It is for young people whose parents are afflicted with alcoholism. You can go there without your parents' permission or knowledge, and it's absolutely free. You will meet friends your age there who have the same problem you face. You will also meet grownups who'll show you how to handle it. I hope you'll give Alateen a call.

God loves you, Karen. I trust that He will help you get through this difficult time of your life, and then you'll learn how wonderful a family can be when drinking does not occur. Until then, keep your faith. Thanks for writing me.

# 14.
## *Angry Women and Passive Men*

*T*here is another classic pattern of marital disharmony occurring so commonly today that I feel I should devote an entire chapter to its cause and effect. Many of you will find yourselves described on the next few pages. Others will recognize parents, friends or perhaps that divorced couple that used to live next door.

The problem has its origins in childhood, long before a young man and woman stand at the altar to say, "I do." For her part, the girl is taught subtly by her culture that marriage is a lifelong romantic experience; that loving husbands are entirely responsible for the happiness of their wives; that a good relationship between a man and woman should be sufficient to meet all needs and desires; and that any sadness or depression that a woman might encounter is her husband's fault. At least, he has the power to eradicate it if he cares enough. In other words, many American women come into marriage with unrealistically romantic expectations which are certain to be dashed. Not only does this orientation set up a bride for disappointment and agitation in the future; it also places enormous pressure on her husband to deliver the impossible.

Unfortunately, the man of the house was taught some misconceptions in his formative years, too. He learned, perhaps from his father, that his only responsibility is to provide materially for his family. He must enter a business or profession and succeed at all costs, climbing the ladder of success and achieving an ever-increasing standard of living as proof of manhood. It never occurs to him that he is supposed to "carry" his wife emotionally. For Pete's sake! If he pays his family's bills and is a loyal husband, what more could any woman ask for? He simply doesn't understand what she wants.

Inevitably, these differing assumptions collide head-on during the early years of marriage. Young John is out there competing like crazy in the marketplace, thinking his successes are automatically appreciated by the lady at home. To his shock, she not only fails to notice, but even seems to resent the work that takes him from her. "I'm doing it for you, babe!" he says. Diane isn't convinced.

What gradually develops from that misunderstanding is a deep, abiding anger on Diane's part, and a bewildered disgust from John. This pattern has been responsible for a million divorces in the past decade. The wife is convinced that her low self-esteem and her unhappiness are the result of her husband's romantic failures. With every year that passes, she becomes more bitter and hostile at him for giving so little of himself to his family. She attacks him viciously for what she considers to be his deliberate insults, and bludgeons him for refusing to change.

John, on the other hand, does not have it within him to satisfy her needs. He didn't see it modeled by his father and his masculine, competitive temperament is not given to romantic endeavors. Besides, his work takes every ounce of energy in his body. It is a total impasse. There seems to be no way around it.

In the early years, John tries to accommodate Diane occasionally. At other times, he becomes angry and they slug it out in a verbal brawl. The following morning, he feels terrible about those fights. Gradually, his personality begins to change. He hates conflict with his wife and withdraws as a means of avoidance. What he needs most from his home (*like the majority of men*) is tranquility. Thus, he finds ways of escaping. He reads the paper, watches television, works in his shop, goes fishing, cuts the grass, plays golf, works at his desk, goes to a ball game—

anything to stay out of the way of his hostile wife. Does this pacify her? Hardly! It is even more infuriating to have one's anger ignored.

Here she is, screaming for attention and venting her hostility for his husbandly failures. And what does he do in return? He hides. He becomes more silent. He runs. The cycle has become a vicious one. The more anger she displays for his uninvolvement, the more detached he becomes. This inflames his wife with even greater hostility. She has said everything there is to say and it produced no response. Now she feels powerless and disrespected. Every morning he goes off to work where he can socialize with his friends, but she is stuck in this state of emotional deprivation.

When a relationship has deteriorated to this point, the wife often resorts to some very unfortunate tactics. She begins to look for ways to hurt her husband in return. She embarrasses him by telling his business associates what a cad he is at home. She refuses to attend office functions or provide any other support for his occupation. She tells stories about him to their church associates. She shuts him down sexually and undermines his relationship with the children. To be sure, she can be a formidable opponent in the art of infighting. No one on the face of the earth could hurt John more deeply than his own wife.

Let me make it clear that I'm not condemning this woman out of hand. She has a good case against her husband. He doesn't meet her needs properly and he's an inveterate workaholic. To that extent, the man is guilty as charged. I attempted to express this feminine perspective in my book *What Wives Wish Their Husbands Knew About Women,* because I believe it is valid.

But every story has two sides, and John's version should also be told. His wife is wrong to believe that her contentment is exclusively his burden. No one should be expected to carry another person emotionally. Only Diane can make herself happy! She has no right to lay that total load on John. A good marriage is one in which the dominant needs are met within the relationship, but where each spouse develops individual identity, interests and friendships. This may be the most delicate tightrope act in marriage. Extreme independence is as destructive to a relationship as total dependence.

To summarize my concern, American women tend to be more unrealistic about marriage than their sisters around the world. Movies and television have made them feel that romantic excitement is not only a birthright, but the most important aspect of marriage. When this "feeling" component of the relationship is missing, the family is doomed. It'll just have to be scrapped. Not even the welfare of the children is important enough to preserve the marriage, and that is tragic.

Let me speak directly and boldly to the women who have seen themselves in this chapter. With all due respect, my most difficult task may be to help you recognize yourselves as part of the problem. The angry women I've counseled in the past have been so consumed by their husbands' disrespect and failures that they couldn't acknowledge their role in his inability to respond. But certainly, they had helped to make him what he was.

Look at it this way. Verbal bludgeoning never made anyone more loving or sensitive. You simply can't tear a guy to pieces and then expect him to meet your emotional needs. He's not made that way. Rather than attacking an unresponsive man and driving him away, there is a method of drawing him in your direction. It is accomplished by taking the pressure off him—by pulling backward a bit—by avoiding the worn-out accusations and complaints—by appearing to need him less—by showing appreciation for what he does right and for being fun to be with. Happiness is a marvelous magnet to the human personality.

Sometimes it is necessary to interject a challenge into the relationship in order to motivate a disengaged spouse. According to the *love must be tough* philosophy, a demeanor of self-confidence, mysterious quietness and independence is far more effective in getting attention than a frontal assault.

I remember counseling a bright young lady whom I'll call Janet. She came to me because she seemed to be losing the affection of her husband. Frank appeared bored when he was at home and he refused to take her out with him. On weekends, he went sailing with his friends despite the bitter protests of his wife. She had begged for his attention for months, but the slippage continued.

I hypothesized that Janet was invading Frank's territory and needed to recapture the challenge that made him want to marry her. Thus, I suggested that she retreat into her own world— stop "reaching" for him when he was at home—schedule some personal activities independently of his availability, etc. Simultaneously, I urged her to give him vague explanations about why her personality had changed. She was instructed not to display anger or discontent, allowing Frank to draw his own conclusions about what she was thinking. My purpose was to change his frame of reference. Instead of his thinking, "How can I escape from this woman who is driving me crazy," I wanted him to wonder, "What's going on? Am I losing Janet? Have I pushed her too far? Has she found someone else?"

The results were dramatic. About a week after the change of manner was instituted, Janet and Frank were at home together one evening. After several hours of uninspired conversation and yawns, Janet told her husband that she was rather tired and wanted to go to bed. She said goodnight matter-of-factly and went to her bedroom. About thirty minutes later, Frank threw open the door and turned on the light. He proceeded to make passionate love to her, later saying that he couldn't stand the barrier that had come between them. It was precisely that barrier which Janet had complained about for months. Her approach had been so overbearing that she was driving him away from her. When she changed her direction, Frank also threw his truck in reverse. It often happens that way.

Having raised the subject of sex, let me ask you an interesting question. Which marriage is likely to enjoy the greatest physical attraction, the steady-as-a-rock relationship or the one that runs hot and cold? Surprisingly, it is the one that varies from time to time. The highest voltage occurs not in the static marriage that is characterized by overfamiliarity, overexposure and demystification. According to Kinsey researchers, the healthiest relationship is one that "breathes"—one that drifts from a time of closeness and tenderness to a more distant posture. That sets up another exciting reunion as the cycle continues. Couples that work or play together day after day are at a disadvantage compared to husbands and wives whose lifestyle takes them apart briefly and then brings them back together.

Do you see the relevance to our discussion? Those individuals who constantly hover over their partners, drawing their complete reason for existence from that one person, actually handicap the relationship. They interfere with the natural "breathing" that proves to be so healthy over the years.

I'll conclude with an enlightening interview with my good friend Jean Lush, respected marriage, family and child counselor. She spoke these words on our radio program, "Focus on the Family."

LUSH:   Over-closeness can cause a marriage to become very dry. When a couple becomes tied to one another in this way, when they feed off each other exclusively, they lose some of the magic. You see, I feel a woman should preserve what I call the "mystique" that is uniquely hers. There should always be a bit of "mystery" in her personality.

DOBSON:   Do you think it is possible for a husband and wife to destroy this sense of mystery by overcommunicating?

LUSH:   I certainly do. I have counseled couples that complained about not loving each other anymore, even though they communicated beautifully. When they told me *how* they communicated, I then understood why love had died. They had destroyed the mystique and left only the bare ugliness. That's why I hate to see absolute honesty in marriage.

DOBSON:   Explain what you mean by that.

LUSH:   Well, let's consider what happens to a woman throughout the menstrual cycle. She can have some pretty depressing days, especially during the premenstrual stage. Speaking personally, I had a very biting, vicious tongue at that time, and that is not unusual. Now, if a woman believes she has a right—even an obligation—to be totally honest even when she knows her perception is distorted, she can say some horrid things that she doesn't really mean. That can be very hard on a marriage. It is simply not healthy to dump all the ugliness on your partner. We need to exercise some discipline in what we say to one another.

DOBSON:   When you say you are opposed to total honesty in a marriage, you're not suggesting that husbands and wives be *dishonest* with one another, are you?

LUSH:   No. But I am saying we don't have to verbalize every thought that comes in our heads. Love is a delicate flower that must be nurtured. It doesn't like heat and it doesn't like cold. Remember that husbands and wives live in fleshly bodies; we are not saints, and too much ugly reality can take the edge off our affection for one another.

DOBSON:   You also worry about women who lean too heavily on their husbands in their thirties, expecting them to carry them emotionally—

LUSH:   I know of no better way to set up a mid-life crisis ten years later than for a woman to demand more of her husband than he can give in his thirties.

I couldn't have said it better myself!

# 15.

# *Loving Toughness for Singles*

**A**n entire book could be written on the *love must be tough* principles as related to unmarried men and women. The problem, quite frankly, is that many singles want so desperately to be married that they violate the laws of freedom and respect in romantic relationships. That is like turning a firehose on a flickering flame. All that remains is black smoke and ashes.

I heard of one young man who was determined to win the affection of a girl who refused to even see him. He decided that the way to her heart was through the mail, so he began writing her a love letter every day. When she did not respond, he increased his output to three notes every twenty-four hours. In all, he wrote her more than seven hundred letters—and she married the postman.

That is the way the system works. Romantic love is one of those rare human endeavors that succeeds best when it requires the least effort. Those who work the hardest at it are the most likely to fail. And speaking of people who try harder, no one beats a dude named Keith Ruff whose story was told in the *Los Angeles Times,* February 21, 1982, by Betty Cuniberti. The headline read, "Man Spends $20,000 Trying to Win Hand of Girl Who Can Say No."

A love-struck man holed up in a $200-a-day Washington hotel has spent, at latest estimate, close to $20,000 demonstrating to his beloved that he won't take "no" for an answer to his marriage proposal.

On bended knee on Christmas Day, 35-year-old Keith Ruff, once a stockbroker in Beverly Hills, proposed marriage to 20-year-old Karine Bolstein, a cocktail waitress at a Washington restaurant. He met her in a shoe store last summer. The pair had gone out a few times over a two-month period before the proposal.

To his proposal, she looked down and said, "No."

Since then, Ruff has remained in Washington and demonstrated his wish that she reconsider by sending her everything but a partridge in a pear tree.

That may be next.

He is, he thinks, "close to spending all of my money. I'm not an Arab sheik."

*Shower of Gifts*

The tokens of his affection include:

—A Learjet, placed on standby at the airport, "in case she wanted to ride around."

—Between 3,000 and 5,000 flowers.

—A limousine equipped with a bar and television, parked outside her door.

—A gold ring.

—$200 worth of champagne.

—Catered lobster dinners.

—Musicians to serenade her.

—A clown to amuse her younger brother.

—A man dressed as Prince Charming, bearing a glass slipper.

—Cookies, candy and perfume.

—Sandwich-sign wearers walking around her home and the restaurant where Bolstein works, conveying the message "Mr. Dennis Keith Ruff LOVES Ms. Karine Bolstein."

—Balloons, which she promptly popped. "What else would she do?" said the undaunted Ruff. "The house was so full of flowers there was no room to walk around."

—For her father, a basket of nuts and $300 worth of cigars "to pass out to his friends at the Labor Department. It may sound goofy, but I like him."

—For her mother, flowers at the French Embassy, where she works. "I don't think her mother likes me. She called the police," Ruff said. "But I'll keep sending gifts to her also. How could anyone be so mad?"

—For both her parents, a stepladder, "so they might look at the relationship from a different angle."

Unsurprisingly, Ruff said he has "a very, very strange monetary situation."

He has not worked in some time, describing himself as being of independent means.

"I don't care how many job offers I get. I'm not interested in any of them," Ruff said. "I'd rather think about her than sit at a job."

He said he will spend his last dime and will beg for money if he has to, that he will "keep on trying for 10 years, 20 years. I'll ask her to marry me 50,000 times."

## Nothing Stops Him

"It doesn't matter how many times she says no. I will do everything in my power that's not absurd or against a reasonable law. I wouldn't stop if she became a nun.

"I've never felt this way before!"

Bolstein, meanwhile, said she is flattered, but too young to get married. She also said the house looks like a funeral parlor.

Ruff said, "I don't want to force her to love me, but I can't stop.

"Maybe this makes her nervous, but at least she gets to smile along with being nervous. Anybody would like it somewhat."

Ruff said many people he talks to are skeptical.

"People would say my love is strange," he said, "but our whole society is falling apart because of the way people love. What is dating? Some guy putting his paws all over you?

"My friends in L.A. know how many women I've gone out with. I didn't like being a womanizer. I believe in the old values. I found the woman I love."

Ruff said he spends a lot of time in his hotel room planning what to do next and occasionally crying. Bolstein, meanwhile, has been getting asked for her autograph where she works and has had a drink there named after her, a concoction of gin, vodka and rum entitled She Won't.

Ruff said Bolstein called him once. "But I hung up on her. I didn't like what she said.

"Reality, to me, is disturbing," Ruff said. "I'd rather close my eyes and see her face.

"Fantasy is where I'm living. I'm living with hope.

"And some very big bills."*

There are several things ol' Ruff needs to know about women, assuming Miss Bolstein hasn't gotten the message across by now. He could cry in his hotel room for the next fifty years without generating the tiniest bit of sympathy from her. And that jet airplane doesn't mean a hill of beans to her either. Very few women are attracted to sniveling men who crawl, who bribe, who whine and make donkeys of themselves in view of the whole world. Tell me, who wants to marry an unambitious weirdo who grovels in the dirt like a whipped puppy? Goodbye, romance! Hello, poorhouse.

On a much smaller scale, of course, the same mistake is made by singles in other places. They reveal their hopes and dreams too early in the game and scare the socks off potential lovers. Divorcees fall into the same trap—especially single women who need a man to support them and their children. Male candidates for that assignment are rarities and are sometimes recruited like All-American athletes. I've seen no better illustration than the following item, also appearing in the *Los Angeles Times*. It was submitted to Virginia Doody Klein for use in her column "Living With Divorce":

Q. I am a recently divorced, professional man with an unusual problem. I hope you can help me. A woman I dated once called me before I even had a chance to make a second date with her and

---

* "Man Spends $20,000 Trying to Win Hand of Girl Who Can Say No" by Betty Cuniberti, copyright, 1982, *Los Angeles Times*. Reprinted by permission.

wanted to know why I hadn't called her again. After our second
date she began to call almost daily with offers for dinner, something funny she'd read and thought I'd enjoy, etc. The crazy
part is that this same routine has started with another woman
I'm just beginning to ask out. If such behavior is typical, maybe
I should have stayed married! How do I extricate myself from
this frenzied dating and have a nice, quiet social life?*

Isn't it obvious what is occurring here? The women being
dated by this "professional man" are chasing him like a hound
after a rabbit. And predictably, his natural impulse is to run.
If they are interested in pulling him toward them, they simply
must not invade his territory. Instead, they should maintain a
sense of decorum in their responses to him.

I attempted to explain the "how to" of this recommendation
during the mid-seventies when I was writing *What Wives Wish
Their Husbands Knew About Women*. The concepts I was formulat-
ing then have withstood intensive scrutiny since that time and
provide the foundation for the book you are reading. This is
what I wrote:

It is of highest priority to maintain a distinct element of dignity
and self-respect in all romantic encounters. I have observed that
many relationships suffer from a failure to recognize a universal
characteristic of human nature. We value that which we are fortunate
to get; we discredit that with which we are stuck! We lust for the
very thing which is beyond our grasp; we disdain that same item
when it becomes a permanent possession. No toy is ever as much
fun to play with as it appeared to a wide-eyed child in a store.
Seldom does an expensive automobile provide the satisfaction anticipated by the man who dreamed of its ownership. This principle is
even more dramatically accurate in romantic affairs, particularly with
reference to men. Let's look at the extreme case of a Don Juan,
the perpetual lover who buzzes from one feminine flower to another.

* *Los Angeles Times*, April 12, 1982. The above excerpt is from the nationally
syndicated newspaper column LIVING WITH DIVORCE by Virginia Doody
Klein © 1982 Sun Features Inc.

His heart throbs and pants after the elusive princess who drops her glass slipper as she flees. Every ounce of energy is focused on her capture. However, the intensity of his desire is dependent on her unavailability. The moment his passionate dreams materialize, he begins to ask himself, "Is this what I really want?" Farther down the line as the relationship progresses toward the routine circumstances of everyday life, he is attracted by new princesses and begins to wonder how he can escape the older model.

Now, I would not imply that all men, or even the majority of them, are as exploitative and impermanent as the gadabout I described. But to a lesser degree, most men and women are impelled by the same urges. How many times have I seen a bored, tired relationship become a torrent of desire and longing the moment one partner rejects the other and walks out. After years of apathy, the "dumpee" suddenly burns with romantic desire and desperate hope.

This principle hits even closer to home for me at this moment. Right now, as I am writing these words, I am sitting in the waiting room of a large hospital while my wife is undergoing major abdominal surgery. I am writing to ease my tension and anxiety. While I have always been close to Shirley, my appreciation and tender love for her are maximal this morning. Less than five minutes ago, a surgeon emerged from the operating room with a grim face, informing the man near me that his wife is consumed with cancer. He spoke in unguarded terms of the unfavorable pathological report and the malignant infestation. I will be speaking to Shirley's surgeon within the hour and my vulnerability is keenly felt. While my love for my wife has never flagged through our fourteen years together, it has rarely been as intense as in this moment of threat. You see, not only are our emotions affected by the challenge of pursuit, but also by the possibility of irrevocable loss. (The surgeon arrived as I was writing the sentence above, saying my wife came through the operation with no complications, and the pathologist recognized no abnormal tissue. I am indeed a grateful man! My deepest sympathy is with the less fortunate family whose tragedy I witnessed today.)

A better example of fickle emotions is illustrated by my early relationship with Shirley. When we first met, she was a lowly sophomore in college and I was a lofty senior. I viewed myself as a big man on campus, and my relationship with this young coed mattered little to me. She, in turn, had been very successful with boys, and was greatly challenged by the independence I demonstrated. She wanted to win me primarily because she wasn't sure she could, but her enthusiasm inhibited my own interest in return. After graduation, we had one of those lengthy conversations well known to lovers the world over, when I said I wanted her to date other fellows while I was in the Army because I didn't plan to get married soon. I'll never forget her reaction. I expected Shirley to cry and hold on to me. Instead, she said, "I've been thinking the same thoughts, and I would like to date other guys. Why don't we just go our separate ways for now?" Her answer rocked me. For the first time in our relationship, she was moving away from me. What I didn't know was that Shirley stoically closed her front door and then cried all night.

I went away to the Army and returned to the University of Southern California for my graduate training. By this time, Shirley was an exalted senior and I was a collegiate has-been. She was homecoming queen, senior class president, a member of *Who's Who in American Colleges and Universities,* and one of the most popular girls in her class. And as might be expected, she suddenly looked very attractive to me. I began to call several times a day, complain about who she was spending her time with, and try to find ways to please my dream girl. However, the moment Shirley saw my enthusiasm and anxiety, her affection began to die. Gone was the challenge which had attracted her two years before. Instead, I had become just another fellow pounding on her door and asking for favors.

One day after a particularly uninspiring date, I sat down at a desk and spent two solid hours thinking about what was happening. And during the course of the introspection, I realized the mistake I was making. A light flashed in my head and I grabbed a pen and wrote ten changes I was going to make in our relationship. First, I was determined to demonstrate self-respect and dignity, even if I lost the one I now loved so deeply. Second, I decided to convey this attitude every time I got the chance: "I am going somewhere in life, and I'm anxious to get there. I love you and hope you choose to go with me. If you do, I'll give myself to you and try to make you happy. However, if you choose not to make the journey with me, then I can't force my will on you. The decision is yours and I'll accept it." There were other elements to my new manner, but they all centered on self-confidence and independence.

The first night that I applied the new formula was one of the most thrilling experiences of my life. The girl who is now my wife saw me starting to slip away on that evening, and she reacted with alarm. We were riding in silence in my car, and Shirley asked me to pull over to the curb and stop. When I did she put her arms around my neck and said, "I'm afraid I'm losing you and I don't know why. Do you still love me?" I noticed by the reflected light of the moon that she had tears in her eyes. She obviously didn't hear my thumping heart as I made a little speech about my solitary journey in life. You see, I had reestablished the challenge for Shirley, and she responded beautifully.

The psychological force which produced our see-saw relationship is an important one, since it is almost universal in human nature. Forgive the redundancy, but I must restate the principle: we crave that which we can't attain, but we disrespect that which we can't escape. This axiom is particularly relevant in romantic matters, and has probably influenced your love life, too.*

Given that background, let me get very specific with those of you who are single but wish not to be. (No insult is intended to those who are single by design and wish to remain unmarried. That is a legitimate choice which should be respected by friends and family, alike.) Listed below are sixteen suggestions that will help you conform to the principles of loving toughness in matters of the heart.

1. Don't let the relationship move too fast in its infancy. The phrase "too hot not to cool down" has validity. Take it one step at a time.
2. Don't discuss your personal inadequacies and flaws in great detail when the relationship is new. No matter how warm and accepting your friend may be, any great revelation of low self-esteem or embarrassing weaknesses can be fatal when interpersonal "valleys" occur. And they *will* occur.

---

* *What Wives Wish Their Husbands Knew About Women*, (Wheaton, IL: Tyndale, House, 1975), pp. 78–82.

3. Remember that respect precedes love. Build it stone upon stone.

4. Don't call too often on the phone or give the other person an opportunity to get tired of you.

5. Don't be too quick to reveal your desire to get married— or that you think you've just found Mr. Wonderful or Miss Marvelous. If your partner has not arrived at the same conclusion, you'll throw him or her into panic.

6. *Most important.* Relationships are constantly being "tested" by cautious lovers who like to nibble at the bait before swallowing the hook. This testing procedure takes many forms, but it usually involves pulling backward from the other person to see what will happen. Perhaps a foolish fight is initiated. Maybe two weeks will pass without a phone call. Or sometimes flirtation occurs with a rival. In each instance, the question being asked is, "How important am I to you and what would you do if you lost me?" An even more basic issue lies below that one. It wants to know, "How free am I to leave if I want to?" It is incredibly important in these instances to appear poised, secure and equally independent. Do not grasp the other person and beg for mercy. Some people remain single throughout life because they cannot resist the temptation to grovel when the test occurs.

7. Extending the same concept, keep in mind that virtually every dating relationship that continues for a year or more and seems to be moving toward marriage will be given the ultimate test. A breakup will occur, motivated by only one of the lovers. The rejected individual should know that their future together depends on the skill with which he/she handles that crisis. If the hurting individual can remain calm, as Shirley did with me, the next two steps may be reconciliation and marriage. It often happens that way. If not, then no amount of pleading will change anything.

8. Do not expect anyone to meet *all* your emotional needs.

Maintain interests and activities outside that romantic relationship, even after marriage.

9. Guard against selfishness in your love affair. Neither the man nor the woman should do all the giving. I once broke up with a girl because she let me take her to nice places, bring her flowers, buy her lunch, etc. I wanted to do these things, but expected her to reciprocate in some way. She didn't.

10. Beware of blindness to obvious warning signs that tell you that your potential husband or wife is basically disloyal, hateful, spiritually uncommitted, hooked on drugs or alcohol, given to selfishness, etc. Believe me, a bad marriage is far worse than the most lonely instance of singleness.

11. Don't marry the person you think you can live with; marry only the individual you think you can't live without.

12. Be careful to defend the "line of respect," even during a dating relationship. A man *should* open doors for a woman on a formal evening; a woman *should* speak respectfully of her escort when in public, etc. If you don't preserve this delicate line when the foundations of marriage are being laid, it will be virtually impossible to construct them later.

13. Do not equate human worth with flawless beauty or handsomeness! If you require physical perfection in your mate, he or she may make the same demands of you. Don't let love escape you because of the false values of your culture. In the same vein, be careful not to *compare* yourself with others—which is the root of all inferiority.

14. If genuine love has escaped you thus far, don't begin believing "no one would ever want me." That is a deadly trap that can destroy you, emotionally! Millions of people are looking for someone to love. The problem is finding one another!

15. Regardless of how brilliant the love affair has been, take time to "check your assumptions" with your partner be-

fore committing yourself to marriage. It is surprising how often men and women plunge toward matrimony without ever becoming aware of major differences in expectation between them. For example:

a. Do you want to have children? How soon? How many?

b. Where will you live?

c. Will the wife work? How soon? How about after children are born?

d. Who will lead in the relationship? What does that *really* mean?

e. How will you relate to your in-laws?

f. How will money be spent?

g. Where will you attend church?

These and dozens of other "assumptions" should be discussed item by item, perhaps with the help of a premarital counselor. Many future struggles can be avoided by coming to terms with potential areas of disagreement. If the differences are great enough, it is even possible that the marriage should never occur.

16. Finally, sexual familiarity can be deadly to a relationship. In addition to the many moral, spiritual and physical reasons for remaining virgins until marriage, there are numerous psychological and interpersonal advantages to the exercise of self-control and discipline. Though it's an old-fashioned notion, perhaps, it is still true that men do not respect "easy" women and often become bored with those who have held nothing in reserve. Likewise, women often disrespect men who have only one thing on their minds. Both sexes need to remember how to use a very ancient word. It's pronounced "NO!"

These sixteen suggestions are not guaranteed to win the hand of a lover, of course, but they will certainly beat the approach of Mr. Keith Ruff. And you'll save $20,000 in the process!

# 16.
## *Components of a Good Marriage*

*P*erhaps we have said enough about deteriorating human relationships and why homes are falling apart today. I have devoted the large measure of fifteen chapters to the concept of loving toughness and how it can draw families back together even when they have been on the brink of disintegration. But there are limitations to this approach, directly related to the inherent strength of the foundation upon which the troubled marriage was built. For the injured partner to show self-respect and poise in a period of crisis will bring about no more than a temporary respite *unless there is a foundation of authentic love upon which to rebuild.*

It is appropriate, therefore, that we turn our attention now to the foundation itself. What are the mysterious ingredients that almost all good marriages have in common? What accounts for the marvelous blending of personalities when two separate and distinct individuals establish a young family and then live together in love and in harmony for the next fifty or sixty years? Is anything of significance known about these long-term marriages that will help others achieve stability in a world of impermanence?

Fortunately, Dr. Desmond Morris has provided an intelligent answer to those questions in his book *Intimate Behaviour*. It was brought to my attention by Dr. Donald Joy, who interpreted the findings for our radio listeners. Dr. Joy said research now verifies that the healthiest marriages are those where a proper "bonding" has occurred between a husband and wife. Bonding refers to the emotional covenant that links a man and woman together for life and makes them intensely valuable to one another. It is the specialness that sets those two lovers apart from every other person on the face of the earth. It is God's gift of companionship to those who have experienced it.

But how does this bonding occur and why is it missing in so many relationships? According to Drs. Joy and Morris, bonding is most likely to develop among those who have moved systematically and slowly through twelve steps during their courtship and early marriage. These stages, described below,* represent a progression of physical intimacy from which a permanent commitment often evolves.

1. *Eye to body.* A glance reveals much about a person—sex, size, shape, age, personality and status. The importance people place on these criteria determines whether or not they will be attracted to each other.

2. *Eye to eye.* When the man and woman who are strangers to each other exchange glances, their most natural reaction is to look away, usually with embarrassment. If their eyes meet again, they may smile, which signals that they might like to become better acquainted.

3. *Voice to voice.* Their initial conversations are trivial, and include questions like "What is your name?" or "What do you do for a living?" During this long stage the two people learn much about each other's opinions, pastimes, activities, habits, hobbies, likes and dislikes. If they're compatible, they become friends.

4. *Hand to hand.* The first instance of physical contact between the couple is usually on nonromantic occasions such as when the man helps the woman descend a high step or aids her across an obstacle. At this point either of the individuals can withdraw from the relationship without rejecting the other. However, if

---

* *Intimate Behavior* by Desmond Morris, chap. 3, "Sexual Intimacy" (New York: Random House, 1971), esp. pp. 73–78. Used by permission.

continued, hand-to-hand contact will eventually become an evidence of the couple's romantic attachment to each other.

5. *Hand to shoulder.* This affectionate embrace is still noncommittal. It is a "buddy" type position in which the man and woman are side by side. They are more concerned with the world in front of them than they are with each other. The hand-to-shoulder contact reveals a relationship that is more than a close friendship, but probably not real love.

6. *Hand to waist.* Because this is something two people of the same sex would not ordinarily do, it is clearly romantic. They are close enough to be sharing secrets or intimate language with each other. Yet, as they walk side by side with hand to waist, they are still facing forward.

7. *Face to face.* This level of contact involves gazing into one another's eyes, hugging and kissing. If none of the previous steps were skipped, the man and woman will have developed a special code from experience that enables them to engage in deep communication with very few words. At this point sexual desire becomes an important factor in the relationship.

8. *Hand to head.* This is an extension of the previous stage. The man and woman tend to cradle or stroke each other's head while kissing or talking. Rarely do individuals in our culture touch the head of another person unless they are either romantically involved or unless they are family members. It is a designation of emotional closeness.

9–12. *The final steps.* The last four levels of involvement are distinctly sexual and private. They are (9) *hand to body,* (10) *mouth to breast,* (11) *touching below the waist,* and (12) *intercourse.* Obviously, the final acts of physical contact should be reserved for the marital relationship, since they are progressively sexual and intensely personal.

What Joy and Morris are saying is that intimacy must proceed slowly if a male-female relationship is to achieve its full potential. When two people love each other deeply and are committed for life, they have usually developed a great volume of understandings between them that would be considered insignificant to anyone else. They share countless private memories unknown to the rest of the world. That is, in large measure, where their sense of specialness to one another originates. Furthermore, the critical factor is that they have taken these steps *in sequence.* When later stages are reached prematurely, such as when couples kiss passionately on the first date or have sexual intercourse before marriage, something precious is lost from the relationship. Instead, their courtship should be nurtured through leisurely walks and talks and "lovers' secrets" that lay the foundation for mutual intimacy. Now we can see how the present environment of sexual permissiveness and lust serves to weaken the institution of marriage and undermine the stability of the family.*

At the risk of trivializing a beautiful concept, let me share the words of a recent popular song that illustrates this shared intimacy. Though the lyrics were apparently intended to be humorous, they speak clearly about the voice-to-voice stage of courtship from which bonded relationships develop.**

I'm the official historian on Shirley Jean Berrell,
I've know her since Lord only knows and I won't tell;
I caught her the first time she stumbled and fell,
And Shirley, she knows me just as well.
I can tell you her birthday and her daddy's middle name,
The uncles on her momma's side and ones they don't claim;
What she's got for Christmas since nineteen fifty two,
And that's only the beginning of the things I could tell you.
I can tell you her fav'rite song and where she'd like to park,
And why to this very day she's scared of the dark;
How she got her nickname and that scar behind her knee,

---

* If you have further interest, let me suggest that you consult Joy's extended work linking pair bonding to Genesis 2 and to Jesus' words in Matthew 19. See "Basic Life Intimacies: Pair Bonding" and "Jesus: What God Joins Together," Tape 8341 in the series *Discipleship Development in the Home 1983.* This is one of sixteen tapes in the series. Write to Center for the Study of Children, Conscience, and the Family, Wilmore, KY 40390.

** Title: The Official Historian On Shirley Jean Berrell. Written by: Don Reid and Harold Reid. As recorded by The Statler Brothers. Copyright © 1978 by American Cowboy Music Company. Used by permission.

If there's anything you need to know 'bout Shirley, just ask me.
I know where she's ticklish and her every little quirk,
The funnies she don't read, and her number at work;
I know what she stands for and what she won't allow,
The only thing that I don't know is where she is right now.
Ole Shirley, she knows me just as well.

It would appear that Shirley Jean Berrell and her singing boyfriend are well on their way toward a bonded relationship. I hope they will be happy together.

Before we tuck away this understanding of bonded commitments, let me emphasize that this concept applies not only to courtship experiences. The most successful marriages are those wherein husbands and wives journey through the twelve steps regularly in their daily lives. Touching and talking and holding hands and gazing into one another's eyes and building memories are as important to partners in their mid-life years as to rambunctious twenty-year-olds. Indeed, the best way to invigorate a tired sex life is to walk through the twelve steps of courtship, regularly and with gusto! Conversely, when sexual intercourse is experienced without the stages of intimacy that should have preceded it in prior days, the woman is likely to feel used and abused.

For couples that have found it difficult to maintain the kind of intimacy and closeness I have described, I would like to offer the strongest endorsement for a program called Marriage Encounter. While not intended for marriages in serious jeopardy, this program is the best I've seen for improving the quality of communication within the family. The principles on which it is based are valid and effective.

Shirley and I had heard about Marriage Encounter for years but had never found time to participate. Finally, at the urging of a pediatrician friend, we decided to experience ME for ourselves. Frankly, I attended for professional reasons, not expecting to get anything relevant to my wife and me. If there is anything I felt Shirley and I didn't need it was help in communicating. I have rarely been so wrong.

The beauty of Marriage Encounter is that it has the ability to *float* to wherever the need is greatest. In our case, the need had little to do with communication in the classic sense. Instead, we discovered a secret source of tension that Shirley had not verbalized and I didn't know existed. It had to do with the recent deaths of eight senior members of our small family, six of whom were males. My wife had watched as the survivors struggled to cope with life alone and the awesome implications of sudden widowhood. Because Shirley and I are now in our mid-forties, she was quietly worrying about the possibility of losing me—and wanting to know where we are going from here. My loving wife was also saying to herself, "I know Jim needed me when we were younger and he was struggling to establish himself professionally. But do I *still* have a prominent place in his heart?"

One simply does not sit down to discuss such delicate matters, voice to voice, in the rush and hubbub of everyday life. They are held inside until (and if) an opportunity to express them is provided. For Shirley and me, that occurred throughout the Marriage Encounter program. In the early part of the weekend, we worked through the possibility of my death then on the final morning, the issue of my continued love for her was laid to rest.

Shirley was alone in our hotel room, expressing her private concern in a written statement to me. And by divine leadership I'm sure, I was in another room addressing the same issue even though we had not discussed it. When we came together and renewed our commitment for the future, whatever it might hold, Shirley and I experienced one of the most emotional moments of our lives. It was a highlight of our twenty-one years together, and neither of us will ever forget it.

Although it will require me to share an intensely personal statement between my wife and me, I would like to conclude with a portion of the letter I wrote to her on that memorable morning. I will skip the more intimate details, quoting only the memories that "bonded" me to my bride.

Who else shares the memory of my youth during which the foundations of love were laid? I ask you, who else could occupy the place
that is reserved for the only woman who was *there* when I graduated
from college and went to the Army and returned as a student at
USC and bought my first decent car (and promptly wrecked it)
and picked out an inexpensive wedding ring with you (and paid
for it with Savings Bonds) and we prayed and thanked God for
what we had. Then we said the wedding vows and my dad prayed,
"Lord, you gave us Jimmy and Shirley as infants to love and cherish
and raise for a season, and tonight, we give them back to you after
our labor of love—not as two separate individuals, but as one!"
And everyone cried. Then we left for the honeymoon and spent
all our money and came home to an apartment full of rice and a
bell on the bed, and we had only just begun. You taught the second
grade and I taught (and fell in love with) a bunch of sixth graders
and especially a kid named Norbert and I earned a masters degree
and passed the comprehensive exams for a doctorate and we bought
our first little home and remodeled it and I dug up all the grass
and buried it in a 10 foot hole which later sank and looked like
two graves in the front yard—and while spreading the dirt to make
a new lawn, I accidentally "planted" eight million ash seeds from
our tree and discovered two weeks later that we had a forest growing
between our house and the street. Then alas, you delivered our
very own baby and we loved her half to death and named her
Danae Ann and built a room on our little bungalow and gradually
filled it with furniture. Then I joined the staff of Childrens Hospital
and I did well there, but still didn't have enough money to pay
our USC tuition and other expenses so we sold (and ate) a Volks-
wagen. Then I earned a Ph.D. and we cried and thanked God
for what we had. In 1970, we brought home a little boy and named
him James Ryan and loved him half to death and didn't sleep for
six months. And I labored over a manuscript titled "Dare To"
something or other and then reeled backward under a flood of
favorable responses and a few not so favorable responses and received a small royalty check and thought it was a fortune and I
joined the faculty at USC School of Medicine and did well there.
Soon I found myself pacing the halls of Huntington Memorial Hospital as a team of grim faced neurologists examined your nervous
system for evidence of hypothalamic tumor and I prayed and begged

God to let me complete my life with my best friend, and He finally said, "Yes—for now," and we cried and thanked Him for what we had. And we bought a new house and promptly tore it to shreds and went skiing in Vail, Colorado, and tore your leg to shreds and I called your mom to report the accident and she tore me to shreds and our toddler, Ryan, tore the whole town of Arcadia to shreds. And the construction on the house seemed to go on forever and you stood in the shattered living room and cried every Saturday night because so little had been accomplished. Then during the worst of the mess, 100 friends gave us a surprise house warming and they slopped through the debris and mud and sawdust and cereal bowls and sandwich parts—and the next morning you groaned and asked, "Did it really happen?" And I published a new book called *Hide or Seek* (What?) and everyone called it Hide *and* Seek and the publisher sent us to Hawaii and we stood on the balcony overlooking the bay and thanked God for what we had. And I published "What Wives Wish" and people liked it and the honors rolled in and the speaking requests arrived by the hundreds. Then you underwent risky surgery and I said, "Lord, not now!" And the doctor said, "No cancer!" and we cried and thanked God for what we had. Then I started a radio program and took a leave of absence from Childrens Hospital and opened a little office in Arcadia called Focus on the Family, which a three-year-old radio listener later called "Poke us in the Family," and we got more visible. Then we went to Kansas City for a family vacation and my dad prayed on the last day and said, "Lord, we know it can't always be the wonderful way it is now, but we thank you for the love we enjoy today." A month later he experienced his heart attack and in December I said goodbye to my gentle friend and you put your arm around me and said, "I'm hurting with you!" and I cried and said "I love you!" And we invited my mother to spend six weeks with us during her recuperation period and the three of us endured the loneliest Christmas of our lives as the empty chair and missing place setting reminded us of his red sweater and domi-noes and apples and a stack of sophisticated books and a little dog named Benji who always sat on his lap. But life went on. My mother staggered to get herself back together and couldn't and lost fifteen pounds and moved to California and still ached for her missing friend. And more books were written and more honors arrived and we became better known and our influence spread and we thanked God for what we had. And our daughter went into adolescence and this great authority on children knew he was inadequate and found himself asking God to help him with the awesome task of parenting and He did and we thanked Him for sharing His wisdom with us. And then a little dog named Siggie who was sort of a dachshund grew old and toothless and we had to let the vet do his thing, and a fifteen-year-love affair between man and dog ended with a whimper. But a pup named Mindy showed up at the front door and life went on. Then a series of films were produced in San Antonio, Texas, and our world turned upside down as we were thrust into the fishbowl and 'Poke us in the Family" expanded in new directions and life got busier and more hectic and time became more precious and then someone invited us to a Marriage Encounter weekend where I sit at this moment.

So I ask you! Who's gonna take your place in my life? You have become me and I have become you. We are inseparable. I've now spent 46 percent of my life with you, and I can't even remember much of the first 54! Not one of the experiences I've listed can be comprehended by anyone but the woman who lived through them with me. Those days are gone, but their aroma lingers on in our minds. And with every event during these twenty-one years, our lives have become more intertwined—blending eventually into this incredible affection that I bear for you today.

Is it any wonder that I can read your face like a book when we are in a crowd? The slightest narrowing of your eyes speaks volumes to me about the thoughts that are running through your conscious experience. As you open Christmas presents, I know instantly if you like the color or style of the gift, because your feelings cannot be hidden from me.

I love you, S.M.D. (remember the monogrammed shirt)? I love the girl who believed in me before I believed in myself. I love the girl who never complained about huge school bills and books and hot apartments and rented junky furniture and no vacations and humble little Volkswagens. You have been *with* me—encouraging me, loving me and supporting me since August 27, 1960. And the status you have given me in our home is beyond what I have deserved.

So why do I want to go on living? It's because I have you to take that journey with. Otherwise, why make the trip?? The half life that lies ahead promises to be tougher than the years behind us. It is in the nature of things that my mom will someday join my father and then she will be laid to rest beside him in Olathe, Kansas, overlooking a wind-swept hill from whence he walked with Benji and recorded a cassette tape for me describing the beauty of that spot. Then we'll have to say goodbye to your Mom and Dad. Gone will be the table games we played and the Ping Pong and lawn darts and Joe's laughter and Alma's wonderful ham dinners and her underlined birthday cards and the little yellow house in Long Beach. Everything within me screams "No!" But my Dad's final prayer is still valid—"We know it can't always be the way it is now." When that time comes, our childhoods will then be severed—cut off by the passing of the beloved parents who bore us.

What then, my sweet wife? To whom will I turn for solace and comfort? To whom can I say, "I'm hurting!" and know that I am understood in more than an abstract manner? To whom can I turn when the summer leaves begin to change colors and fall to the ground? How much I have enjoyed the springtime and the warmth of the summer sun. The flowers and the green grass and the blue sky and the clear streams have been savored to their fullest. But alas, autumn is coming. Even now, I can feel a little nip in the air—and I try not to look at a distant, lone cloud that passes near the horizon. I must face the fact that winter lies ahead—with its ice and sleet and snow to pierce us through. But in this instance, winter will not be followed by springtime, except in the glory of the life to come. With whom, then, will I spend that final season of my life?

None but you, Shirls. The only joy of the future will be in experiencing it as we have the past twenty-one years—hand in hand with the one I love . . . a young miss named Shirley Deere, who gave me everything she had—including her heart.

Thank you, babe, for making this journey with me. Let's finish it—together!

Your Jim


*That* is known as marital bonding!

# 17

# With More Love
# to the Victims

*I* began this book with an expression of love and empathy for the men and women who have gone through severe family crises and personal suffering. I would like to conclude my comments by speaking directly to those same individuals who desperately need the advice I've offered. I know this has not been an easy book for you to read. Frankly, I found it difficult to write. I have taken no pleasure in describing the sordid details of infidelity, child and wife abuse, homosexuality, alcoholism, marital conflict and divorce. But this is reality! Half the American couples over forty years of age have experienced extramarital affairs at some point,* and more divorces are occurring than marriages at this time. That translates into millions of people who have experienced the same emotional trauma that you've encountered. And that's why I wrote this book. I hoped to provide some practical tools and philosophies with which to draw your partner back in the direction of commitment and responsibility. I pray that will happen!

But now I must offer one final word of advice, equal in importance to anything I have written. Surprisingly, my greatest concern is reserved for those families that have pulled themselves back from the brink of divorce with God's help and seem to

---

* According to *Psychology Today*, 1983.

be on the road to recovery. At that moment of celebration, a new peril often emerges that can be more deadly than the first. Just when the battle appears to have been won, everything can be lost for reasons that did not exist in the beginning. That's why I urge you to read this final chapter carefully and heed its warning.

In order to explain, let's return to the plight of Linda, whose husband is involved with another woman. As you recall, she has suffered untold agonies over Paul's blatant infidelity and rejection, being wounded almost to the point of death. Indeed, suicide has undoubtedly been her option many times in the early hours of the morning or on a lonely afternoon.

But then a quiet transformation begins to occur. Let's suppose Linda stumbles across the principles of loving toughness and gradually learns to set her husband free. She realizes for the first time that the guilt she feels is not entirely valid, and the dynamics of their conflict come into clearer focus. Her self-esteem slowly returns and the long bleak winter starts to thaw.

You can't imagine how good it feels for her to escape the pain of the past! Relief, blessed relief, occurs after months of unrelenting depression and sorrow. But beware! Therein lies the danger! It is very easy in that moment for Linda to forget her original desire to draw Paul back to her, permanently sealing him out of her heart. When the selfishness of what he has done is fully realized, her depression can turn to anger or profound apathy. She could also fear that once Paul has returned and the crisis is over, her original problems will recur and life will be no different from their darkest hours. For these and other reasons, Linda may no longer want Paul back when she finally learns she can have him. It often happens just that way! When it does, the unfaithful spouse sometimes goes through the same agonies that besieged his wife a few months earlier. The entire relationship can turn upside down.

To all those who find yourselves in Linda's situation today, I urge you to remain open to the will of the Lord, even though it means loving and forgiving the one who caused so much grief! I know it is easier to talk about forgiveness than to exercise it, especially when the hurt was inflicted by a marital partner. Nevertheless, that is what we as Christians are required to do in time. There is no place for hatred in the heart of one who has himself been forgiven of so many sins.

I must stress this point. The toughness I have recommended in response to irresponsibility can be destructive and vicious unless it is characterized by genuine love and compassion. Our purpose must never be to hurt or punish the other person, even when retribution is deserved by him or her. Vengeance is the exclusive prerogative of the Lord (Rom. 12:19). Furthermore, resentment is a dangerous emotion. It can be a malignancy that consumes the spirit and warps the mind, leaving us bitter and disappointed with life. I'll say it again: no matter how badly we have been mistreated or how selfish our partners have seemed, we are called upon to release them from accountability. That is the meaning of true forgiveness. According to psychologist Archibald Hart, "Forgiveness is surrendering my *right* to hurt you for hurting me."

Some of the most dramatic moments in my counseling experience have involved outright forgiveness by one spouse for the devastating wrongs of the other. I'll never forget the day Janelle walked into my office. She brought an air of depression and sadness with her as she sat head downward in a chair. Her husband, Lonny, had asked for my help after Janelle attempted suicide in the middle of the night. He had gotten up at 3:00 A.M. to go to the bathroom and found her in the process of taking her life. If he had not awakened, she would have been gone.

Lonny had no idea why Janelle attempted to kill herself or why she was so depressed. She wouldn't tell him. He knew she was dealing with something awesome but he could not make her reveal it. Even after the suicide episode, she held everything inside, moping around the house in depression. Finally, she agreed to talk to me and Lonny brought her to my office.

Lonny sat outside while Janelle and I talked. At first she threw a smokescreen around her emotions, but eventually the story broke. She was deeply involved in an affair with a business acquaintance and the guilt was tearing her to pieces.

I said, "Janelle, you know that the only way you will ever settle this matter is to confess the affair to Lonny. You can't keep this enormous secret between you forever. It will be a barrier that will destroy what's left of your marriage. I think you should tell Lonny the truth and seek his help in ending the affair."

She looked at me sadly and said, "I know that's right, but I can't tell him! I've tried and I just can't do it!"

I said, "Do you want *me* to do it?"

Janelle nodded through the tears, and I said, "Go to the waiting room and ask Lonny to come in. You stay there and I'll call for you in about an hour."

Lonny arrived with an anxious look on his face. He was worried about his wife, yet he had no idea what to expect. That was, I believe, one of the toughest assignments I've ever had—to tell a loving, faithful husband that he had been betrayed by his wife. As might be expected, the news hit him like a blow from a hammer. His anger and anguish were intertwined with compassion and remorse. We continued talking for a while and then I invited Janelle back into my office.

These two wounded people sat in depression as I attempted to ease communication between them. But the atmosphere was extremely heavy. Finally, I prayed and asked them to leave and come back at 10:00 A.M. the next day.

Janelle and Lonny had a bad night. They didn't fight, but they were both so hurt and disturbed that they couldn't sleep. Nor could they talk to one another. They arrived back in my office the next morning in the same state in which they had left. I talked to them about forgiveness, about divine healing of memories and about their present situation. I don't know how it happened even today, but a spirit of love began to permeate that office. We prayed together and suddenly, Janelle and Lonny fell into each other's arms, weeping and asking for forgiveness and *granting* that forgiveness. It was an unbelievable moment of joy for all three of us, and it happened because a man who had been deceived and betrayed was willing to say, "I hold nothing against you!"

Though this kind of forgiveness is difficult to either give or receive, I can assure you that divorce is even more difficult. It leaves scars on its victims that will last a lifetime. This is why God hates divorce (Mal. 2:16). He knows the devastation that it inflicts not only on adults, but even more severely on young children! That is, of course, the soft spot in my heart. I have a special tenderness for kids who hurt, especially those who ache for the arms of a departed parent. It is an everyday occurrence among children in the United States. Over half of the boys and girls under eighteen years of age have one or both parents missing. Within three years of the divorce, half of the fathers never see their children. One of those kids, Lisa Castro, a friend of my daughter, wrote the following poem and addressed it to her father. She said,

Father, I wonder . . .
Did you want to leave us?
I've always wondered why.
Did you ever wonder how it *could* have been?
Did it ever make you cry?
I sit at home and think of you—and how our lives could be.
I've always wished, so very much, that you were here with me.
I feel like a part of me has somehow never grown.
Do you ever think of me? My father? My own?

I don't know the circumstance which caused Lisa's father to leave, but often the motive for family disintegration is nothing more substantial than unbridled selfishness. In those instances, I must ask what sexual thrills—what romantic extravaganzas, what conflict—could justify the pain of a child like Lisa? It will be remembered for a lifetime! Comedian Jonathan Winters referred to his parents' divorce forty years earlier when he said, "All of my humor is a response to sorrow!"

Divorce is also devastating to parents who want to be with the children they lost in a custody hearing. That is Martin's situation, as he described it in an emotional letter to me:

Dear Dr. Dobson:

I watched your film on the subject of fathering last night. Those around me were in tears when it was over and I could not find the strength to leave. You see, I am the father of a 3½-year-old son named Bradley. Two years ago his mother decided to divorce me and she got a court order to force me out of the house. A staff psychologist testified that I would make a better parent than my wife, but she got custody of the child and the judge gave her almost everything we had. The one thing I wanted—the one thing I really cared about—was little Bradley. He needed me!

Bradley was still in diapers when my wife and I separated and the only words he could say were, "My daddy!" But he knew what they meant. When I would come for my visitation day, he would cling to me saying those words. He would sleep for three hours within a few minutes after I picked him up. Then when I returned him to his mother, Bradley would stretch his arms toward me screaming, "My daddy! My daddy!"

I have cherished my times with Bradley these past two years. He and I watch television together and he lies on my stomach and goes to sleep. Sometimes he sits on the floor beside me and puts his little legs on top of me because Daddy puts his feet on the couch. I taught Bradley to brush his teeth and how to use the potty chair. If he's had a bad dream he will tell me about it. In earlier days when his mother washed his hair, Bradley would scream. But now I tell him what I expect and assure him that I will not get soap in his eyes, and he doesn't cry. He trusts me. I feel so close to my son. If I go to the garage and do some work, Bradley goes with me. Daddy is so proud to have his little boy with him that he doesn't even care when his son dumps nails all over the floor. I taught him to pray.

Now that Bradley is three and a half, he can express his feelings to me. Yesterday he asked if I had to take him back to be with his mommy. When I told him, "Not right now, son, but yes, this is the day," he started crying. He said, "Daddy, I really miss you." Yes, I cried then, too. And I am crying now.

Bradley's mother tells him I am no good and he should forget me. She criticizes the meals I fix and tries to convince him that I can't cook. She curses me and calls me names in Bradley's presence. These are minor offenses compared to other things she has done. But the most painful thing to me is that my child has a daddy to teach him only four days a month. Four lousy, stinking, rotten days! How can I mold his developing personality and teach him my values in four short days?

Bradley, I love you. My prayers for you and those like you never cease. I'll take my four days with you now and pray for the time I can see you more.

You can understand, Dr. Dobson, why I was screaming inside when I saw your movie tonight. I wanted you to keep saying it. Tell the people what they are doing to their kids! Show them how to resolve their differences. Save the families.

It doesn't seem quite right for a 6'2", 205-pound Black Belt in karate to cry, but that's all I seem to do anymore.

> Thanks for your time,
> Martin

It almost seems as though Singer Tom T. Hall had a father like Martin in mind when he wrote the lyrics to his song, "I Left You Some Kisses On The Door."

Your mom says I can't see you; the judge says that it's right.
We can't be together, 'cause me and Mommy fight.
But you're my little girl and Daddy loves you more and more.
And I left you some kisses on the door.

I came by to see you but Mommy just said no.
I knocked but Mommy saw me as she peeked through the hole.
I only want to hold you, honey; Mommy thinks it's war.
But I left you some kisses on the door.

You know your Daddy worries, honey, but it's not Mama's fault.
You do what your Mommy says; you know she's the boss.

No matter what I gave you, Mommy thought you needed more,
But I left you some kisses on the door.

Hey, you're my little angel, babe, and it don't make much sense
To only get to watch you play through that old schoolyard fence.
Someday you'll come to me, sweetheart, that's all I'm waiting for,
'Cause I left you some kisses on the door.*

Come on, America. Enough is enough! We've had our dance
with divorce and we have a million broken homes to show
for it. We've tried the me-philosophy and the new morality
and unbridled hedonism. They didn't work. Now its time to
get back to some old-fashioned values, like commitment and
sacrifice and responsibility and purity and love and the straight
life. Not only will our children benefit from our self-discipline
and perseverance, but we adults will live in a less neurotic world,
too!

But I can hear someone saying, "Okay, so divorce is not
the answer. I have done everything I can to forgive my mate
but I still don't think I can ever feel affectionate toward this
person who deliberately broke my heart." Let me assure you
that romantic love and tenderness *can* be nurtured back to health
even when the relationship seems beyond the grave. I've seen
the Author of Love "restore the years the locusts have eaten"
for those who have tried to obey Him. I'll conclude with a
letter from Jacque, who has been where *you,* the reader, may
be today.

Dear Dr. Dobson:
    I was married to a non-believer for fourteen years in what proved
to be a living hell on earth. There's no way I can describe how
terrible Brent treated me during that time. I considered running
away or anything that might help me cope. It seemed that my prayers
and my church work were useless in bringing me peace of mind.
Gradually, I gave in to the advances of another church member.

---

* Written by Tom T. Hall. Published by Hallnote Music. Copyright 1979.
All rights reserved. Used by permission.

He was also unhappily married and inevitably, we became deeply involved in an affair.

This man's wife then died of heart disease and I intended to divorce my husband to marry him. But when Brent saw that he was losing me with no hope of reconciliation, he quietly gave up all the terrible treatment of me and became kind almost overnight. He even changed occupations to give him more time at home.

That put me in a very difficult situation. I loved the other man and felt I couldn't live without him and yet I knew it was wrong to divorce my husband. By an act of sheer faith, I broke off the relationship with the other man and did what I believed to be right in the eyes of God. For three years, I did not feel *anything* for my husband. I claimed the scriptures and believed that if I would do what they said, the Lord would give me what I had never had. I admit that I went through a terrible struggle with my emotions at this time.

During the last two years, however, God has poured out a blessing on us that you can't believe! I am so committed to my husband that I find myself loving the man that I hated for fourteen years. God has given me this intense affection for him. Now, something else has happened. Our children have grown so close to us and love each other as never before. We love to look in the Scripture for things to obey and then we make a commitment to do what we've read. First it included a daily study of the Word and now it involves church work—together. We are a witness to all those who see this incredible change in our family.

I said all that to say this. It is worth *everything* to follow God's will even when it contradicts our desires. Oh, there's always the temptation to chuck it from time to time. But I'd rather spend five minutes in real fellowship with the Lord than a lifetime in fun and games. I can truly say, it works!

Thank you,
Jacque

It will work in your family, too. Thanks for reading my book. I pray that the Lord will bless your home with love and warmth and every good thing.

# CHRISTIAN HERALD ASSOCIATION AND ITS MINISTRIES

**CHRISTIAN HERALD ASSOCIATION,** founded in 1878, publishes The Christian Herald Magazine, one of the leading interdenominational religious monthlies in America. Through its wide circulation, it brings inspiring articles and the latest news of religious developments to many families. From the magazine's pages came the initiative for CHRISTIAN HERALD CHILDREN and THE BOWERY MISSION, two individually supported not-for-profit corporations.

**CHRISTIAN HERALD CHILDREN,** established in 1894, is the name for a unique and dynamic ministry to disadvantaged children, offering hope and opportunities which would not otherwise be available for reasons of poverty and neglect. The goal is to develop each child's potential and to demonstrate Christian compassion and understanding to children in need.

*Mont Lawn* is a permanent camp located in Bushkill, Pennsylvania. It is the focal point of a ministry which provides a healthful "vacation with a purpose" to children who without it would be confined to the streets of the city. Up to 1000 children between the age of 7 and 11 come to Mont Lawn each year.

Christian Herald Children maintains year-round contact with children by means of a *City Youth Ministry.* Central to its philosophy is the belief that only through sustained relationships and demonstrated concern can individual lives be truly enriched. Special emphasis is on individual guidance, spiritual and family counseling and tutoring. This follow-up ministry to inner-city children culminates for many in financial assistance toward higher education and career counseling.

**THE BOWERY MISSION,** located at 227 Bowery, New York City, has since 1879 been reaching out to the lost men on the Bowery, offering them what could be their last chance to rebuild their lives. Every man is fed, clothed and ministered to. Countless numbers have entered the 90-day residential rehabilitation program at the Bowery Mission. A concentrated ministry of counseling, medical care, nutrition therapy, Bible study and Gospel services awakens a man to spiritual renewal within himself.

These ministries are supported solely by the voluntary contributions of individuals and by legacies and bequests. Contributions are tax deductible. Checks should be made out either to CHRISTIAN HERALD CHILDREN or to THE BOWERY MISSION.

**Administrative Office: 40 Overlook Drive, Chappaqua, New York 10514**
**Telephone: (914) 769-9000**